LAST POST AT MHOW

BY THE SAME AUTHOR

H.M.S. Captain

ARTHUR HAWKEY

Last Post at Mhow

JARROLDS

JARROLDS PUBLISHERS (LONDON) LTD
178–202 Great Portland Street, London W1

AN IMPRINT OF THE HUTCHINSON GROUP

London Melbourne Sydney
Auckland Bombay Toronto
Johannesburg New York

*

First published 1969

This book has been set in Bembo, printed in Great Britain on Antique Wove paper by Anchor Press, and bound by Wm. Brendon, both of Tiptree, Essex

09 089940 7

Contents

Illustrations

Between pages 84 *and* 85

In the text

The people in the story

6th Inniskilling Dragoons

Lieutenant-Colonel T. R. Crawley
Captain Thomas Smales
Surgeon Gavin Ainslie Turnbull
Assistant Surgeon Oliver Barnett
Major J. E. Swindley
Captain R. W. Renshaw
Regimental Sergeant-Major John Lilley
Clarissa Lilley, the R.S.M.'s wife
Troop Sergeant-Major Wakefield
Troop Sergeant-Major Duval
Lieutenant T. J. Fitzsimon, Adjutant

Commander-in-Chief, British Army

Field Marshal H.R.H. the Duke of Cambridge

Commander-in-Chief, Indian Army

General Sir Hugh Rose (later Lord Strathnairn)

Commander-in-Chief, Bombay Army

Lieutenant-General Sir William Mansfield (later Lord Sandhurst)

Commander of the Mhow Division

Major-General F. T. Farrell

Rifle Brigade

Colonel Sir Alfred Horsford

Legal advisers to Lieutenant-Colonel Crawley

Mr W. Vernon Harcourt, Barrister (later Sir William Harcourt, M.P. Home Secretary)

Mr Waller, Barrister

Mr A. R. Cocker, Solicitor

Deputy Judge Advocate

Mr Denison

The 6th Inniskilling Dragoons was formed by King William III in 1689 and was merged in 1922 with the 5th Inniskilling Dragoons to form the 5/6 Dragoons. In 1927 the regiment was renamed the 5th Inniskilling Dragoon Guards: headquarters Belfast.

Author's preface

This is a true story which caused a tremendous outcry in press and parliament a century ago.

The Royal United Service Institution librarian's tolerance over my indefinite retention of irreplaceable records made this first account of it possible.

The principal characters in this book left no mark upon the history of their time: their impact was upon each other only. Their story creates a cameo of life in the Indian Army when British rule in India was at its peak. I trust that it was not typical; but it happened.

Court-martial procedures have changed since the injustices related here took place, and an accused person may now be properly represented by counsel, as in a civil court.

In reconstructing two lengthy courts martial a great deal of condensing has been necessary, but the main structure of each trial has been retained so that the reader may perhaps form a personal opinion upon the evidence submitted.

No dialogue has been invented: it is all either on record or is accurately implied by remarks which have survived.

I am indebted to Officer Cadet Vinay Kumar Tevatia, of the Indian Army, and to Mr Joseph A. L. Noah, who, quite independently, searched for and found the tomb of Regimental Sergeant-Major John Lilley at Mhow, and described it to me; and to Captain R. N. Dhawan and Lieutenant-Colonel Na Salick, VrC, of the Indian Army, who both photographed the tomb.

I am also obliged to Mr Frank Moraes, editor of the *Indian Express*, whose publication of a letter from me put me in touch with these voluntary helpers.

I also thank the grandchildren of Captain Smales—Mrs

Margaret Yelland and Mrs Riette Beck of Brisbane, and Mrs Joyce Loveday of Melbourne, who kindly supplied the personal details of their grandfather's life in Australia.

Mr T. C. Bray, editor of the *Courier-Mail*, Brisbane, published a letter from me which led me to the Smales family.

As ever, officials in the Public Record Office, the India Office library and British Museum have been most helpful.

A.H.

Bickley
Kent

I

Incident of the 'scarlet woman'

MUTINY is an evocative word. It at once conjures up a picture of violence, revenge and retribution; the unleashing of forces that have hitherto been suppressed, or controlled; the sweeping away of the established order of things and the denying of rule to those who have been accustomed to command and obedience.

In India in the 1860's the word had a particularly sinister association, for the bloodiest uprising in the history of British colonial rule was still of recent memory.

This fact may have affected the judgment of those principally concerned in the Mhow court martial, a shameful and forgotten episode in the annals of the British Army, but one that aroused public opinion to an extraordinary and understandable degree as a tale of military oppression, apparent indifference to human suffering, and scheming in high places was revealed in the newspapers of the day and in parliament.

The story concerns the 6th Inniskilling Dragoons. The background is the horse-lines of this cavalry regiment; and its parade ground, first at Ahmednugger in the Deccan, and then at Mhow where it transferred in November 1861.

The time when the story begins and when it reaches its tragic climax is April and May: high summer, when the sun bores straight down and the air is drawn hot and stifling into the lungs. The rains have not yet come.

Throughout the night of 24–25 April 1861 Lieutenant-Colonel T. R. Crawley, lately commanding officer of the 15th Hussars in England, travelled the seventy miles from Poona to Ahmednugger, east of Bombay, where he was to take command of the 6th Inniskilling Dragoons.

After a journey of some sixteen hours Colonel Crawley and his party, including his wife and mother-in-law, reached the Inniskilling lines about 9.30 a.m., tired, hot and hungry: they had not eaten since 6.30 p.m. the previous night.

Apart from a brief acquaintance of one of the Inniskilling officers as a boy in England many years before, Crawley was a stranger to all the officers in his new regiment.

This makes the curious incident of the colonel's breakfast the more difficult to understand.

Soon after arriving at Ahmednugger Colonel Crawley sent for the officers' mess servant and asked for breakfast to be served to him in his quarters; that is to say, his house.

The messman went away but did not return. Colonel Crawley appears to have been a man of rather short temper at the best of times, and after a night on the road it may be supposed that he was not inclined to wait long in patience for his breakfast.

He despatched his own batman to the mess to find out why the meal was taking so long. The man returned to tell the colonel that breakfast was ready, but that there were no knives and forks available.

The colonel's own cutlery was in his baggage, which had not yet arrived.

The batman was said to have approached the President of the Mess Committee, a Captain J. E. Swindley, for permission to borrow cutlery for the colonel and his family, but he was told it was not possible owing to a mess rule that tableware should not be taken out of the mess.

In fairness to Colonel Crawley at this stage of acquaintanceship with him, it is difficult to understand how, if the account was true, an officer could have been so discourteous to a newly-arrived commanding officer; or why a standing rule, obviously designed to prevent loss of mess knives and forks from haphazard borrowings, should not have been waived.

Colonel Crawley considered it 'a very extraordinary occurrence in the case of the arrival of a new commanding officer . . . who might reasonably expect a little civility and attention from his officers'.

There is no evidence that Captain Swindley—veteran of

the Kaffir War of 1852–3, the Crimea, the Indian Mutiny—had ever fallen out with the colonel before, but it is a fact that he was the only officer—the boy in England—whom Crawley had previously met.

It is also a fact that when the whole tragic story of Colonel Crawley and the 6th Inniskilling Dragoons unfolded itself Swindley swore that he was never approached on behalf of the colonel on this morning, and that he knew nothing whatever of the incident of his breakfast until much later—months afterwards.

His word on this point was accepted by His Royal Highness, the Duke of Cambridge, Commander-in-Chief of the British Army, but he was never believed by the Commander-in-Chief, India, Sir Hugh Rose.

It is quite possible that he did not personally know of the new colonel's breakfast difficulty: it is possible that, although the batman may have told Colonel Crawley that it was by order of the President of the Mess Committee that knives and forks could not be borrowed, in fact the refusal may have come from no higher source than another batman in the regimental mess.

Nevertheless, trivial though the incident was compared with what was to follow in the weeks ahead, it was an inauspicious beginning to the new era of command in the regiment.

Colonel Crawley sent his servant to borrow cutlery elsewhere and it was obtained from the home of a married officer who lived nearby.

At last, about 11 a.m., breakfast was served to the colonel and his family.

Although the 6th Inniskilling Dragoons had a high reputation as a regiment in England, and it was a fashionable one to hold a commission in, the regiment that was the centre of the extraordinary scenes to come was not exactly the same body of men, except in name, as was known in England. This fact had an important bearing on the course events were to take for, so far as the general public in England were concerned, the Inniskillings were unchanged by their passage to India.

But Colonel Crawley did not find the regiment reached his own standards for a crack cavalry regiment. He had been a cavalryman since entering the army as a youthful cornet of sixteen in 1834 and now, at the age of forty-four, nothing but the highest display of military efficiency in horses, officers and men would do for him as a commanding officer.

In his general orders his officers were soon able to read what he thought of them professionally. He slated them for, in his opinion, not knowing how to ride; he asserted that the captains of troops were far more interested in their perquisites than in the efficiency of their horses and men; and the language in which he censured them audibly for their unsoldierly ways came as something of a surprise to them. They had not been accustomed to such an authoritarian manner from their previous commanding officer, Colonel Shute, who had been inclined to judge an officer more by his social background and breeding than by his professional accomplishment.

But the soldierly shortcomings of his officers were not their only faults in Colonel Crawley's eyes. He found their private lives, their social ways, if anything, worse to contemplate.

The officers' mess was in danger of splitting over a 'scarlet woman', as she might have been called in those days. The matter was referred to—when later, in court, it had to be—as the regiment's 'moral and social' difficulty.

It concerned the wife of one of the officers, Mrs Renshaw, wife of Captain Renshaw. When Renshaw first joined the regiment his attractive wife had been very popular and for a time joined willingly in the social life of the station.

The Renshaws had been very friendly with the former commanding officer, Colonel Shute, and he particularly recommended the Renshaws to Crawley as socially acceptable.

As may be well understood, the strict proprieties of the period were even more minutely observed in the introverted society of an Indian-based military establishment. It therefore came as a shock to the Victorian ladies of the 6th Dragoons to learn that Mrs Renshaw had been the guilty party in a lurid divorce hearing.

The facts, briefly, were that a young woman, born Eleanor Ann Johnson in 1829, was orphaned and became a Ward of Chancery. At the age of twenty-one, in December 1850, she married a thirty-five-year-old solicitor named John Joseph Tourle.

After living in London for four years they moved to Woolwich where the young Mrs Tourle met a twenty-one-year-old army lieutenant, Richard Renshaw. It was not long before the young cavalryman became her lover.

There was a brief interlude in their passion in 1857—or it may have been discretion on the part of Mrs Tourle—when she and her husband became reconciled; but she soon returned to the arms of the lieutenant.

Mr Tourle became aware of what was going on and parted from his wife. Seeking evidence of adultery, he and a relative surprised the lieutenant and Mrs Tourle at breakfast in the London Hotel, in Albemarle Street, where they had been staying together.

Divorce proceedings followed, but before he granted Mr Tourle a divorce, the judge, Lord Campbell, made some very strong remarks about the lady who subsequently became Mrs Renshaw. He pointed out in his summing-up that: 'at the very time when she was instituting proceedings in this court for restitution of conjugal rights, she was carrying on an adulterous intercourse with her paramour at the London Hotel'. Such profligacy, Lord Campbell hoped, was of very rare occurrence. The jury found Mrs Tourle guilty of adultery and her husband was granted a divorce.

The outraged feelings of the respectable maids and matrons of the regiment when the news of Mrs Renshaw's past reached their outpost of Empire may be imagined.

The married officers and their spouses—or some of them—closed their ranks to this wanton in wife's clothing who had penetrated their unsuspecting society.

The senior and most articulate of the married officers was Captain Thomas Smales, the fifty-one-year-old regimental paymaster: and Captain Smales had an ally in Captain Gavin Ainslie Turnbull, at thirty-five the senior of the two regimental doctors.

Captain Smales had been on very friendly terms with the new colonel at first, and had taken the not injudicious step of placing his house and servants at the disposal of the new commanding officer on his arrival, until the colonel could make his own domestic arrangements. It appears to have been Captain Smales who came to the rescue of the Crawleys when they were without the means to eat their breakfast.

But this happy relationship received a fatal blow soon after Colonel Crawley assumed command, when Smales felt it his duty to let the colonel know about the Renshaws' past and the feeling of the 'respectable' married officers and their ladies.

Smales later described his action in these words: 'I communicated to Lieutenant-Colonel Crawley facts with which I was personally cognisant, facts that were openly spoken of, namely that Mrs Renshaw's moral antecedents, and Captain Renshaw's conduct in connection therewith, rendered her an undesirable association in the domestic circles of the regiment.'

Colonel Crawley considered the matter for a few days and then sent for Captain Smales and Dr Turnbull at his quarters. There, before three other officers, he gave them a dressing down. He accused them of spreading abroad a very questionable report and said the gossip was utterly groundless.

He even went so far as to remark that if he were to examine the old regimental papers that were kept in an official tin box—what he called his predecessor Colonel Shute's 'legacy' to him—the characters of very few of the officers would survive the investigation.

This naturally annoyed Smales and Turnbull still further; for they were certain there was nothing to their detriment in the old tin box, whatever there might be concerning the younger, more headstrong officers.

There had, in fact, been a number of regrettable incidents among the officers since the regiment's arrival in India. The details, which were recorded in the tin box, will be considered later in the story.

Neither Smales nor Turnbull was a man who could accept censure of this kind, and on such a subject, with good grace. The high moral attitude which they adopted towards the Renshaws showed a lack of charity even when allowance is made for the social background of the times in which they lived; and Colonel Crawley's own character may be judged a little on the entirely different attitude that he displayed.

Smales, since the colonel would not act on 'rumour', sent to England for copies of *The Times* in which the Tourle divorce action was reported.

Meanwhile, neither Captain Smales nor his wife was seen at regimental parties, the odium of mixing with the Renshaws being too much for Mrs Smales—or perhaps merely her husband—to contemplate.

Some understanding of Captain Smales' attitude towards the Renshaws is possible if his own background is taken into account.

He was born in London in 1811, the son of a sea captain, and entered government service as an acting Ordnance clerk in Sierra Leone during the temporary absence of the permanent clerk. Smales was in this position from 1830 to 1833.

He then returned to England to negotiate further official employment, and lived at 1 Chatham Place, Walworth, London, while he applied for a commission—an ensigncy—in the Royal African Colonial Corps. From the references he submitted at this time it can be seen what kind of young man of twenty or so that he was.

Officers under whom he had served in Sierra Leone described him as 'zealous, active, intelligent'; 'extremely zealous'; 'zeal, high character and conduct'.

It will be noted that zeal came into every reference. He was early showing signs that everything with which he had to do must be correctly done and according to regulation.

Mr Smales purchased his commission for £450 on 20 May 1833. He served in the African colonies until 1842. Towards the end of this service he fell in love with the daughter of General George Macdonald, veteran of Waterloo and Governor of Sierra Leone.

Smales and Clara Sarah Macdonald were married in Freetown in 1842.

It was possibly a social advancement for Smales—at least in the colony—to be married to the Governor's daughter. General Macdonald, a soldierly, dignified figure characterised by the specially made high collar that he wore to hide an ugly wound he received at Waterloo, was, of course, the most important man socially in the territory. His son-in-law naturally took his place in the grandeur surrounding the governorship.

What kind of woman his wife was is not known, but it may be assumed that she had the high standard of dignity and conduct associated with senior service families a century ago.

If she was outraged at the idea of mixing socially with a woman who had been publicly branded as immoral, it would not be surprising in view of her background and probable upbringing.

In due course the newspapers arrived from England and Smales and Turnbull, seething no doubt with self-righteous indignation, submitted in writing to Colonel Crawley the proof of the Renshaws' guilt. They demanded nothing less than the expulsion of the Renshaws from regimental society.

The colonel considered the matter again for a day or two and then wrote a memorandum on the subject, giving his considered opinion and decision. This memorandum, dated 9 August 1861, was read out to the Inniskilling officers in the orderly room, and in the presence of a Brigadier Smith, who had been carrying out an inspection of the regiment's riding ability.

The colonel's view was that none of the officers' wives, with the exception of Mrs Smales, had boycotted regimental parties, and the conduct of Captain Renshaw and his wife since Colonel Crawley had joined the regiment had been 'perfectly unexceptional and unimpeached by anyone'.

For these reasons he ruled that he would not be acting in the interests of the harmony of the regiment, or as a Christian if he were now 'to rake up past unhappy incidents in another regiment' and, acting on the advice of Dr Turnbull and Captain Smales, to expel the Renshaws and thereby ruin the career of one and involve both in misery.

It is not difficult to imagine the demeanour of Captain Smales on this occasion: to see his eyebrows rise in feigned astonishment; to hear the snorts of contempt with which he probably punctuated the colonel's reasoned and charitable pronouncements.

That he did behave in a noticeably disapproving fashion is known from a record of what the visiting Brigadier Smith said at the time. The brigadier had been observing Captain Smales and, as the officers were leaving the orderly room after the memorandum had been read, he asked Colonel Crawley to recall Smales for a moment.

The brigadier told the paymaster: 'If I am ever called upon to make a report, or give my opinion about this matter, I should feel it my duty to state that your manner during this meeting has been highly objectionable, and far from what I would be prepared to accept from you myself.'

The colonel, in the course of his memorandum, also forbade Smales and Turnbull to speak of the matter again, and anyone in the camp who did refer to the Renshaw scandal thereafter was socially ignored by Crawley and his family.

In the formal, repetitive social life of an army station the inevitable result of this was that the commissioned ranks of the 6th Inniskilling Dragoons became divided socially into the pro-Renshaws and the anti-Renshaws.

But there was more than just the Renshaw scandal to divide Colonel Crawley from his officers. They resented his 'new broom' methods from the start.

Some indication of the feeling towards him within only a fortnight of his arrival may be seen in the odd affair of the mess wines.

On the other hand, it may equally be evidence of the unfriendly, ill-mannered and defiant attitude adopted by some of the officers on too short an acquaintance of their new commanding officer, and evidence too of the decline in quality of the 6th Dragoons' officers at this time.

Between the departure of Colonel Shute and the arrival of Colonel Crawley the regiment was temporarily commanded by Captain Weir, former regimental sergeant-major in the Inniskillings.

During this short interval between commands the regiment was inspected by the brigade commander, Brigadier Hobson. It was a foot parade in full dress and the brigadier was not satisfied with the men's turn-out. He wrote officially of his dissatisfaction and another inspection was arranged for 6 May, within a fortnight of Colonel Crawley's taking command.

That the colonel was somewhat displeased with an adverse

report having been made on his new command goes without saying. As he accompanied the brigadier round the barracks his displeasure increased at what he considered to be untidiness of the rooms. He also thought that the sergeants' mess was dirty and that the sergeant in charge was drunk.

It appears that some of the untidiness—that of storing the men's bags of grooming equipment under the mess tables—was a custom in the regiment. But it was not the kind of thing Colonel Crawley had been used to in England.

'I had come red hot from the strictest garrison known in the United Kingdom,' he was later to tell a court martial, 'where for upwards of a year I had held command of one of the finest regiments of cavalry in the British service.'

Captain Weir had already started a train of trouble in the higher command by protesting at the adverse report made by Brigadier Hobson, and requesting a further inspection by higher authority. He put in both a defence and denial of the brigadier's strictures and proved himself to be a man not willing to take criticism uncomplainingly. No doubt, having risen from the ranks, and finding himself a temporary commanding officer while still of junior rank, he was more sensitive than usual to the personal slur a bad report involved.

On Weir's insistence the matter went to the major-general commanding the Division, and then to the Commander-in-Chief, India. The C.-in-C. wrote a letter censuring Weir and telling him to be more careful about insubordinate complaints in future; but Weir took it as being a letter for form's sake only and, since no further action was taken against him, some sort of justification for his complaint.

But it brought the Inniskillings, not for the first time, to the notice of the high command in none too favourable a light.

On the day of the second inspection by the brigadier, Colonel Crawley asked Captain Swindley, the thirty-one-year-old President of the Mess Committee, to invite Brigadier Hobson and his staff to dinner at an early date.

Swindley bridled at this, and pointed out that this second inspection was regarded as a sort of punishment parade, and that there had already been two half-yearly inspection dinners and he, Swindley, objected to paying for any more.

Colonel Crawley, angrily no doubt, told him:

'It is an army order that an inspecting or reviewing general should dine at the mess so that he may be able to report on the economy and management of the mess. Brigadier Hobson must be asked to dine, no matter how many previous mess entertainments the officers have given.'

Swindley stubbornly replied that if that was so then he could not be compelled to supply any but the usual mess wines, port and sherry, at dinner.

The colonel simply answered: 'Let champagne and claret, then, be put on the table, and charged to me.'

The brigadier was duly dined and Colonel Crawley paid for the additional wines.

2

Decline of a regiment

To UNDERSTAND Colonel Crawley's position in the 6th Inniskilling Dragoons, and some of the events that occurred during his command, it is necessary to know things that were completely unknown to the general public at the time, and unknown to the press and members of parliament who attacked him with, it seemed, every justification.

What was the truth about the famous regiment to which he came unsuspecting, and unsuspected, on that April morning in 1861?

There were two things not generally appreciated: first, it was not realised how a regiment could be altered in character by transfer to India; and, secondly, no one except a limited number of high-ranking officers in India knew that trouble among the officers of the Inniskillings had begun long before Colonel Crawley arrived upon the scene. Consequently, when the regiment achieved notoriety the new commanding officer was seen by the public as the principal reason for it.

Most of the cavalry regiments in England in mid-Victorian times were officered by men of some wealth, and with sporting interests. The 6th Inniskilling Dragoons, that had fought at Waterloo, Balaclava and Sevastopol, was no exception. Its officers included some with influential and titled family connections. They were the kind of officers whom Colonel Shute, the former commander, admired and desired in his regiment.

But when the unit was ordered to India the prospect was not altogether pleasing to some of these officers, and they arranged—as was not unusual—to transfer to other regiments remaining at home. The well-known heat and disease of India was not something they were prepared voluntarily to exchange for the hunting shires of England and the round of London society.

During the months before leaving the regiment it is possible that these transferring officers may have lost some of their interest in the military community that would soon cease to be their home; and it is also possible that these tiny eroding particles of indifference may, even before the regiment sailed, have begun the unsuspected deterioration of discipline and morale that was to be exposed fully only when Colonel Crawley took command.

The officers who joined the regiment in India in 1858 were, according to Sir Hugh Rose, the Commander-in-Chief, India, 'not of the same station in society, habits or pursuits as those who had served in the regiment at home'. It was not that Sir Hugh Rose was a snob, particularly, but he was pointing out that the officers were drawn from a wider social background than formerly and a wise, strong and impartial man was needed at their head to weld them into an harmonious whole.

But not only the officers were changed. The need to make the Inniskillings up to establishment for transfer to India involved the posting of 'a large number of volunteers—mostly bad characters—from other units in Great Britain'.

It is well known that commanding officers do not willingly release their best men when another regiment needs making up to strength, but they are seldom known to go to great lengths to obstruct the transfer of their undesirables.

And so there was a general dilution of quality from top to bottom of the regiment.

One of the officers who joined the Inniskillings in India was an Anglo-Indian—Cornet Revell. For some reason, the younger officers made a butt of Revell, and the more senior members of the mess did little or nothing to stop them.

When goaded to a certain point Revell gave way to strong language and on one occasion, after Captain Charles Thesiger, twenty-eight-year-old son of the first Baron Chelmsford, had thrown fruit at him in the mess, a fight broke out between Revell and several officers. One, a Captain Hardy, was knocked out by Thesiger.

A court of enquiry followed and Colonel Shute was warned by the Commander-in-Chief that if matters did not improve he might be relieved of his command.

The divisional commander, now Sir Henry Somerset, ordered the Inniskillings' officers' mess to be closed at 11 p.m. each night.

Sir Henry also commented on the court of enquiry: 'Cornet Revell's character has been rather harshly represented by Colonel Shute when he states that Cornet Revell has been habitually coarse and vulgar in his expressions, as the evidence before the court proves the contrary.'

The fact was that, since the regiment's arrival in India, Colonel Shute had been utterly dismayed at what he considered to be a falling off in the social standing of his officers. The admission of a eurasian officer to regimental society only chafed the raw graze left upon his patrician mind by the other changes that had taken place.

However, it appears that the family advantages enjoyed by Captain Thesiger did not prevent his behaving like an ill-mannered hooligan towards a less privileged member of the mess. It was probably an incident that Lieutenant-General the Hon. Charles Wemyss Thesiger, as he eventually became, preferred to forget.

Sir Hugh Rose summed up Colonel Shute in this way: 'Colonel Shute has a weakness: he has ideas of social exclusiveness incompatible, I think, with those of any society, particularly military society; incompatible also with that strict impartiality which is indispensable for the exercise of command, and of the requisite influence over the heterogeneous elements to be found amongst the officers of a cavalry regiment transferred to India.'

Sir Hugh regarded the closure of the mess at 11 p.m. as 'a mark of displeasure with a body of officers, and a want of confidence in them of which I do not remember a parallel'.

Colonel Shute 'entertains the mistaken idea that the credit of his regiment would be increased by its being composed, as much as possible, of officers of birth, or of good social position; and he certainly gave way to a tendency to show more countenance to officers of this, rather than of a humbler class.

'By so acting he forewent the advantages which result from a commanding officer making military merit and good conduct the sole claim to his favour; and he lost the personal influence which as much as, and even more than official authority, enables a commander to prevent misconduct amongst his subordinates, or to settle without heart-burnings or unfavourable notoriety, difficulties which will occur occasionally in all societies.'

Adverse reports were made on the regiment by inspecting generals in both 1859 and 1860 and although things improved in the mess with the despatch of Revell and Thesiger to duties in China, there is no doubt that the dissentions and frictions were still there when Colonel Crawley took command.

This then was 'the legacy' to which Colonel Shute had perhaps ironically referred when he handed over to Colonel Crawley the box of records concerning the regiment's officers.

Having for so long had a commanding officer whose lack of impartiality and judgment had tended to cause disharmony in the regiment, its officers found the iron hand of Colonel Crawley little to their liking either.

There were a series of annoyances to Crawley in the form of petty quarrels between officers which so exasperated him on one occasion that he told them things were settled in a very different way when he had been a young soldier. This oblique reference to duelling, which had been illegal in the army for many years, could not have been meant seriously; but it had its repercussions.

Apart from these domestic shortcomings in the regiment Colonel Crawley—himself a highly efficient soldier—found much to be desired in the military standards of his new regiment.

To take a typical example, there were no properly prepared lines for the horses at Ahmednugger. They stood on bare level ground and when the monsoon came it would become an unhealthy quagmire. This had been foreseen by Colonel Shute, but it appears that, although he had reported the problem, no permission for expenditure of money had come from higher command.

Colonel Crawley took it upon himself to make use of a large balance in the regiment's litter fund* to start improving the horse lines immediately. When, unexpectedly, he was

* Money derived from the sale of manure and stable refuse.

ordered to remit the whole of the litter fund to the Quarter Master General, he managed to convince his superiors that he ought to be allowed to keep half the fund for improving the horses' standing conditions. So there was no longer a financial bar to the improvements.

Crawley ordered the horse lines to be reconstructed so that they sloped; rainwater would then run away from the horses and their standing ground would remain properly drained in the wet season.

He hounded his officers to get this work done in time; and he upbraided them for the delapidated state of the horse-lines equipment—the worn and non-uniform halters.

The captains of troops in those days received an allowance for the maintenance of their line gear and, of course, the less they spent the more they had left for themselves.

The colonel insisted on the equipment being renewed; and his insistence, since it involved a financial outlay, did not make for better relations. His manner of speaking, if not the actual language, was often that of a drill sergeant with a recruit squad. His officers did not like it.

The colonel was to say later: 'Even with all my urgent representations, and all my anxiety, and all the personal superintendence I gave to their construction, the slopes of the lines were not fit to receive the horses till about a fortnight after the rains commenced, and I can safely say that, but for my continued exertions, the health of both men and horses would have suffered most severely during the last monsoon, which I was informed was the heaviest that had been experienced at Nugger during the past twenty years.

'The ground at the end of the lines where the troops paraded was literally a bed of mud in which the horses sank up to their knees and hocks, and such would have been the state of the lines themselves had I not constructed the hard slope for the horses to stand upon.'

This background is given because it shows the kind of general military situation with which Colonel Crawley had to deal, and it is to his credit. Much of what followed was not to his credit, but it is right that he should be seen at the outset as a conscientious, efficient, if not particularly tactful officer.

3

A captain's challenge

THE smouldering acrimony over the Renshaw affair flared up briefly on the afternoon of 6 November 1861, although the incident was not directly connected with the original cause of the trouble; but it illustrates how personal relationships were allowed to interfere with military duties.

On this day Captain Renshaw discovered he had not sufficient cash in hand to complete paying his troop. On applying to the paymaster's office for more money he was refused it.

Smales sent out a note to his clerk in the outer office saying that whoever it was wanting money, he was too late and would have to wait until the next paying-out day, which would have been two days later. There can be little doubt that Smales knew perfectly well which officer was applying for money.

Had it been anyone but Renshaw, Smales would probably have acted differently, but he had already had a brush with Renshaw over regimental money. On an earlier occasion Renshaw had claimed he was five rupees short in a bag of cash issued to him, and Smales had made it up.

On receipt of Smales' note Renshaw went straight to the colonel and complained. Colonel Crawley wrote to Smales directing him to 'pay immediately to Captain Renshaw the amount in full due to him on account of his troop'.

It was now 5 p.m. and Renshaw found that Smales had gone out for his regular evening drive. By the time he returned and was presented with the colonel's note it was 7 p.m. The pay office had been locked by the clerk, and all records put away.

Smales sent a note to the colonel regretting that owing to the lateness of the hour it was not possible to issue money to Captain Renshaw.

From what will be learned of Captain Smales, there can be little doubt that he took some pleasure in not carrying out the colonel's instruction.

Colonel Crawley's immediate reaction was to send an officer to inform Captain Smales that he was under arrest for refusing to obey orders.

Smales, militant at once, despatched a note in reply saying that he would not consider himself under arrest. As an officer, there was no question, in simple arrest, of physical detention; but merely the acceptance of the fact and confinement to the camp area.

But Smales quoted a regulation: 'A paymaster on a foreign station, charged with misdemeanour in the execution of his duty, may be suspended by the officer *commanding-in-chief* on the station; but by no other authority on the station.'

It was a ridiculous contention for, if applicable in such a case, would have placed a regimental paymaster outside the ordinary disciplinary control of his commanding officer—except by reference to the Commander-in-Chief.

Nevertheless, Smales' place was empty at the mess table that night, when another inspecting general was being entertained.

There had, of course, to be a court of enquiry before any further action could be taken against Smales.

The fact that Smales had the excuse of the locked office and the cash box being in the charge of the guard—a fact into which the colonel had not enquired before ordering his arrest—enabled the Commander-in-Chief, Bombay district, Sir William Mansfield, to order Smales' release. It was probably not a course that he took with any great enthusiasm for, apart from the general facts about the regiment with which he must have been familiar, he had received a number of unofficial complaints about Captain Smales, from Colonel Crawley, on previous occasions—the result of the enduring feud between the two men.

Smales' point to the court of enquiry had an air of reasonableness about it: 'If Colonel Crawley had given the matter one moment's reflection he would have known that by waiting until morning, a reference and demand of a reasonable character could have been made to me.'

Smales was an infuriating subordinate who thought he knew exactly how far he could go in challenging his superiors without actually endangering himself, and the irascible Colonel Crawley had only made things worse by his impetuous handling of the situation.

Sir William Mansfield rejected Smales' claim to be outside his colonel's power of arrest, but he considered 'the whole proceedings to have been hurried and ill-judged on the part of the commanding officer. Considering the position of Captain Smales in the regiment; the hour of the day on which Captain Renshaw made his report; the perfect satisfaction which Colonel Crawley had always experienced in the performance of Captain Smales' *official* duties, as stated by himself in evidence (Smales had been careful to bring that out at the enquiry) it was surely for him, as commanding officer, to have given himself time for reflection and further enquiry before proceeding to the extreme step of placing an officer of high regimental position and responsibility in arrest on account of an *ex parte* report'.

Smales was also found wanting by Sir William. Smales was of a militant disposition, well-versed in Queen's Regulations, and was clearly articulate and shrewd in official court proceedings, to say the least.

But success in the courts is a heady mixture for the amateur, and he who experiences it may be lured back, like an inebriate, to savour its exhilaration again.

Captain Smales was undoubtedly pleased at having come through the court of enquiry unscathed. He had shown some forensic ability in his questioning of witnesses. He was not to know, of course, that his vigorous defence had not commended itself to the Commander-in-Chief who, in a confidential report to the Adjutant General in London, wrote: 'the highly objectionable tone adopted by Captain Smales in his defence on the court of enquiry did not escape me, and it is evident to me that that officer has a very slender appreciation of the position of a subordinate in Her Majesty's service with regard to the ordinary rules of discipline.'

Smales had been careful not to go too far in his feud with Crawley. Indeed, Sir William Mansfield had paid a kind of tribute to his skill in this direction in his report: 'It is apparent . . . that he will permit his insolence to his commanding officer to proceed to the utmost tether, when he thinks that circumstances may admit of such conduct with impunity.'

This spicy piece of regimental news did not go unnoticed by the local press, and in view of the important part the newspapers of India and England were to play in the subsequent history of Colonel Crawley and Captain Smales, we may here consider the kind of unbridled reporting and comment that was customary at the time.

The *Deccan Herald*, after a lengthy account of the incident of the cash for Captain Renshaw's troop, went on to say:

'We have no hesitation in stating that in our opinion Captain Smales has been illegally arrested, and the whole affair reflects no credit upon either the commanding officer or upon the captain who made the complaint.

'We are aware that Lieutenant-Colonel Crawley succeeded one of the best and most popular cavalry officers in the service, and therefore had rather uphill work before him, but it only required tact on his part to gradually maintain a position in the regiment equal to that of his predecessor; which position we confidently state can never be gained by a persistence in the line of conduct marked out by his unwarrantable behaviour in the case of Captain Smales.'

So Colonel Crawley was already marked out for unfavourable opinion in this preliminary skirmish with Smales, and no doubt the writer of the despatch was supplied with his inside story by Smales' friends, if not by Captain Smales himself.

Towards the end of 1861 the Inniskillings moved from Ahmednugger to Mhow, a fortified station about 250 miles north-east of Bombay.

Smales made his first mistake in his dealings with Crawley at Mhow on 26 January 1862 when, possibly in a spirit of reprisal for the strict watch kept by Crawley on his official activities, he wrote direct, and improperly, to the War Office in London.

'I feel it to be my duty', he wrote, 'to notify for the information of the Right Honourable, the Secretary of State for War, that the present commanding officer of the 6th Dragoons,

Lieutenant-Colonel Crawley, is not in the habit of regularly attending, personally, the monthly muster of the regiment.

'I do not make this notification as any complaint, merely with a view to my own protection, and a matter of duty, in the case of future reference, it being laid down in the "Explanatory Directions" that the commanding officer's presence . . . is indispensable at the regimental monthly muster.'

Owing to the slow communications of the time this somewhat dangerous letter was not to have its effect for several months; and by that time the feud between Smales and Crawley would have moved on to its tragic consequences.

Petty squabbles continued between Crawley, Smales and Dr Turnbull, and Crawley made various reports on them to higher authority. It amounted almost to a state of persecution of the two men by Crawley, aided in his surveillance of their every official activity by those officers who sided with him most in the 'moral and social' difficulty.

At last, on 26 February 1862, driven beyond endurance it seems, Captain Smales wrote an official letter to Colonel Crawley describing the various annoyances offered to him and requesting that his letter be forwarded to the higher command.

Smales complained that his daily proceedings were closely watched; any careless words were taken down discreetly by the colonel's agents—his brother officers—and whenever he was found to have transgressed regulations or regimental orders in the slightest degree the colonel framed charges as grave as possible against him, as if he had been found out in some deliberate and serious breach of the Articles of War.

Captain Smales must have known that he was taking a risk in complaining about his commanding officer, for 'kicking against the pricks' is not a course generally to be recommended in military life. However, he might have avoided any serious repercussions to himself had he not gone further; but he did. He referred—for the first time to Crawley direct—to the subject of his secret note to the War Office.

Captain Smales' letter reminded the colonel that he, too, was in the habit of contravening regulations in small matters. For example, wrote Captain Smales, Colonel Crawley was often absent from muster parades at which he nevertheless signed returns showing himself to be present.

He also said in his letter: 'It is with respectful regret I remark that your sentiments, expressed on more than one occasion to officers under your command, have been anything but of a conciliatory tendency. You have expressed your regret that the days of duelling were not in existence. Such sentiments, I respectfully think, are not such as either to establish concord or forbearance, have a most unfortunate tendency when in addition to a tone and style of address harsh and unusual, leaving little hope that when offence has been committed, apology or explanation would prove acceptable.'

This letter, couched around with respectful regrets as it was, could only be regarded as insubordinate. It really left Colonel Crawley no alternative but to acknowledge its truth and his own unfitness to hold his command; or, to take up the challenge.

Nevertheless, it was a difficult decision he had to make. There had been trouble enough in the regiment and he must have felt himself to be somewhat on trial as to the extent to which he could improve the conduct and bearing of the Inniskillings. A virtual official revolt by a fairly senior officer could hardly be regarded by anyone as an improvement.

The colonel pondered over the letter for three weeks, and took no official action on it. During this time his recently appointed second-in-command, Lieutenant-Colonel Prior, tried without success to get Captain Smales to withdraw his letter.

Smales very likely regarded this unofficial intervention by Colonel Prior as a sign of weakness on Crawley's part: he stood firm, confident in his initiative.

Finally, when it was quite certain that Smales would not retract, Colonel Crawley handed the letter on to Major-General Farrell, an elderly and somewhat infirm Indian Army officer who was in command of the Mhow station. General Farrell forwarded the letter to Lieutenant-General Sir William Mansfield, Commander-in-Chief in Bombay.

Here the first unusual aspect of the handling of the case can be seen. Mansfield had distinguished himself during the Indian Mutiny and had had the task of reforming the shattered Bengal native army afterwards. It may be that he was hypersensitive to any suggestion of insubordination.

It would have been correct procedure for him to order a court of enquiry to see whether sufficient grounds existed for Captain Smales' complaints and then, if they appeared to have some substance, he could have ordered a court martial upon Colonel Crawley, when it would have been Smales' responsibility to prove his charges.

If, on the other hand, the court of enquiry found that there were not sufficient grounds for complaint against Colonel Crawley, then it would have been proper for Captain Smales himself to face a court martial for having, possibly, written an insubordinate letter.

This course was not followed. Instead, Sir William Mansfield ordered that Smales be tried by court martial on three charges of 'conduct highly insubordinate, most disgraceful, unbecoming the character of an officer and a gentleman, and to the prejudice of good order and military discipline' in having made false and malicious accusations against his commanding officer. Crawley was ordered to prosecute.

Thus, General Mansfield, having been given merely a private and *ex parte* account of the situation by Colonel Crawley, prejudged the issue by the very terms in which the charges were framed. Without any enquiry beyond Colonel Crawley it was alleged in three separate charges that Smales made 'the following false and malicious statement'.

The 'false and malicious statements' were that Crawley had absented himself from obligatory muster parades at the beginning of each month; that he had nevertheless reported himself as having been present; and that he had expressed his regret that the days of duelling were no longer in existence.

It is known that Sir William Mansfield was by this time aware of the antagonism between Captain Smales and Colonel Crawley, but it was no excuse for failing to observe the correct procedure and denying Smales a court of enquiry into his complaint.

It is the 'false and malicious' ingredient of the charges which shows how Colonel Crawley's mind was working. There is no doubt that Captain Smales' letter was insubordinate, and he would almost certainly have been convicted on a simple charge of insubordination.

But the charge was not so simply drawn for a simple reason —a statement may be insubordinate yet be perfectly true. It was essential from Colonel Crawley's point of view that Smales' allegations be judged to be untrue.

The literally fatal court martial assembled at Mhow on Tuesday, 1 April 1862.

4

A captain on trial

THE court to try Captain Thomas Smales consisted of fourteen officers—four lieutenant-colonels, one major, and nine captains. The President of the Court was Lieutenant-Colonel W. Payn of the 72nd Highlanders.

The issue to be decided by the court was a narrow one: it had to find whether, on two occasions, 1 May 1861 and 1 January 1862, Colonel Crawley had or had not been present at the regimental muster parade.

The question of Colonel Crawley's having recommended duelling as a desirable way of settling officers' disputes was a comparatively simple matter, and ought to have been settled on the testimony of Colonel Crawley himself in his opening address for the prosecution.

Dealing with this charge, he said: 'Certain quarrels which were the reverse of creditable to parties concerned . . . had been referred to me for arbitration as their commanding officer. . . . I took occasion to observe on the unseemliness and impropriety of such conduct passing between officers of the same regiment, and remarked that when I was a younger man, and when I first entered the service, such matters were settled in a very different way than by appealing to the commanding officer. I informed the disputants that in those days officers settled matters between themselves when they quarrelled and did not trouble their commanding officer with their disputes. I said I was almost tempted to wish that those days were still in existence, for that then officers would be restrained, if by no higher motive, by a fear of consequences, from the use of gross and improper language towards one another. . . . I have no recollection of ever having made use of the word "duelling" in my remarks, though doubtless my remarks pointed in that direction.'

It may be thought that this was a fairly frank statement of what probably happened. Crawley said he had no intention of recommending duelling; but it was obvious that such an interpretation of his remarks by the officers who heard him was quite justified, and, in fact, almost inevitable.

This allegation of Smales' then was clearly not false.

Captain Smales protested at once that the proceedings were not legal because 'all charges preferred against an officer are to be previously examined by superior authority'.

There was no doubt about the existence of this regulation. It was designed to prevent the unnecessary assembling of courts martial, and the expense and waste of time involved.

The system was rather like a magistrate's court hearing in civil life: a court of enquiry would hear the charges and the evidence, and upon its finding it would be decided whether or not there was a *prima facie* case for trial by court martial.

By the ignoring of this procedure, and presumption without enquiry that a captain's word was not to be taken against his colonel's, Captain Smales was changed from an accuser into an accused, and Colonel Crawley became transformed from an accused into a prosecutor, the charge in its simplest terms being that Captain Smales was a liar.

Having listened to a long statement by Smales the court considered the matter and dismissed the objection. They even found his protest objectionable in itself because they considered it reflected on the conduct of the Commander-in-Chief, the divisional commander and Colonel Crawley, who were jointly responsible for the prosecution in the form it took.

As the proceedings continued it became increasingly apparent that the court was determined to show every consideration to Colonel Crawley and considerably less to Captain Smales.

Smales made a number of objections to procedure and to the general conduct of the case which might have been considered valid and reasonable, but almost without exception they were overruled. Many questions which Smales wanted to ask witnesses were ruled inadmissible or irrelevant. No doubt some of them were, but it would not have been inconsistent with justice had some concessions been made to him, as the accused.

But Smales took the precaution of insisting that a record be made in the proceedings of every protest and every question he asked which was overruled.

Later, when the trial was the subject of lengthy correspondence between India and the War Office, Colonel Payn, the president of the court, tried to justify the trial by claiming that Colonel Crawley had had just as many irrelevant questions overruled by the court but he had not insisted that they be recorded on the proceedings. The transcript of the trial of Captain Smales shows a few questions, comparatively, by Colonel Crawley were overruled and were in fact recorded. Colonel Payn's recollection may have been correct, and there may have been many other questions overruled and not recorded, but there seems no reason why some of Colonel Crawley's questions should be on record and a greater number not noted by the court reporter at all. It is just one of the many unsatisfactory aspects of the Mhow court martial.

Colonel Crawley's reply to Smales' charges that he was absent from the parades in question was to assert that he *was* present, or present in the sense that he was in the parade area.

His witnesses, seven in number, included Lieutenant W. W. Bennitt, the regiment's twenty-three-year-old musketry instructor, whose evidence was curious to say the least.

Dealing with the muster parade on 1 May, Colonel Crawley asked the lieutenant:

'Did you see me there during the time the roll of troops was being called in the vicinity of the column?'

Yes, the lieutenant had seen the colonel there at this time.

Lieutenant Bennitt even recalled precise details.

'How far was I from the column, and whereabouts as regards the column, in the front or on the left flank?' asked Crawley.

'As far as I can recollect, towards the left front of the column and close to it.'

'Did I appear to be looking at the details of the muster as it was being taken—that is—observing the calling of the roll, and filing of the troops to water afterwards?'

'I recollect, with reference to the filing of the troops to water, the remarks made by Colonel Crawley about the appearance of the horses, and the length of the hair on their legs. Colonel Crawley might have been present at the calling of the roll without my seeing him. I was paying attention to the filing of the men.'

Lieutenant Bennitt answered further questions about the colonel's dress.

Finally, Crawley asked him:

'Do you recollect my going into the horse lines of Captain Weir's troop, of which you were subaltern, and speaking about the long hair on the horses' legs after the muster of 1 May?'

'I recollect perfectly,' answered the lieutenant.

Anyone listening to the lieutenant's evidence could have had little doubt that here was a man who was on parade on 1 May and clearly remembered seeing his colonel there; a man who could also recall perfectly remarks his commanding officer had made on that occasion.

It was the custom of the time for accused officers to be allowed the benefit of professional legal advice, but lawyers were not permitted personally to examine witnesses. In this respect military courts lagged far behind the civil law.

At courts martial the fiction was maintained that an officer defended himself. In fact, he was allowed to have a solicitor or barrister at his elbow prompting him as to the form or line of questioning, but the accused actually examined the witness himself.

It, of course, placed an accused man at a disadvantage when dealing with an awkward or adroitly reluctant witness.

Captain Smales rose to cross-examine. He may perhaps be pictured pausing in silence for a moment or two, eyeing the lieutenant, reluctant almost to reveal the trump card he held.

'Be so good as to peruse the Regimental Order now produced, and copy of Brigade Order, both dated 30 April 1861, the former detailing you as a member of a board at 6 a.m. 1 May. State to the court whether you attended that board.'

No doubt this preamble with its dangerous implication alerted and perhaps disconcerted the lieutenant.

Cautiously, he replied:

'I was a member of a board when I first went to Nugger. I don't recollect this particular board. . . .'

Smales went straight to the point:

'How can you account for being on a muster parade when ordered on committee duty?'

'I have no recollection of the committee duty,' Lieutenant Bennitt persisted, 'but I recollect the parade.'

'You have sworn you were on the muster parade on 1 May 1861. Are you now prepared to swear that you were not on the committee ordered to assemble at 6 a.m. on the morning of the muster parade?'

The lieutenant held his ground, though he might possibly have welcomed its opening to swallow him at this moment.

'To the best of my recollection, I was not . . .'

Smales left the matter for the moment, and asked another question aimed obviously at further confounding the lieutenant when Smales judged the moment to be right.

'As regards your troop, in what position were you placed when you saw the colonel?'

'In the right front of my troop.'

Another seemingly clear recollection of the disputed parade.

It was Tuesday, 8 April, and the court adjourned until the following Friday.

Faced with a direct contradiction of his evidence, and the certain knowledge that Captain Smales must have proof of his true whereabouts on 1 May, and would eventually produce it, Lieutenant Bennitt did some hasty checking himself.

He telegraphed to Nugger and found that he had, in fact, signed the proceedings of an audit board, as one of its members, on 1 May, so it was clear that he could not have been on parade observing Colonel Crawley at the same time.

He came into court at the resumed hearing on 11 April 1862 and asked permission to make a statement about his previous evidence. He had discovered, he told the court, that apart from his serving on an audit board on 1 May, there had been a parade on 30 April too, 'of which I have not the slightest recollection . . . but as both these parades were in general watering order, and on two consecutive days, a thing of rare occurrence and *both exactly alike*—with the exception of the roll call—I think I may have been mistaken in my date: that is, I may have mistaken the general watering parade of 30 April for the muster parade of 1 May. . . . I would therefore beg the court to allow me to qualify my answers to the questions put to me on Tuesday last with the expression "to the best of my belief", or to allow me to retract my evidence altogether with reference to the muster parade of 1 May.'

Captain Smales naturally seized upon this embarrassment to the prosecution by handing in a written protest to the court against the explanation of Lieutenant Bennitt's evidence. He would no doubt have preferred to regard Bennitt more as a liar than as someone who had made a mistake that happened to be vital to his case. Such an interpretation of Bennitt's mistake would have carried with it the innuendo that his evidence, and possibly that of other prosecution witnesses, had been concocted with Crawley.

But Colonel Crawley, although impetuous, short-tempered and lacking in judgment in many ways, was not dishonest. Perhaps it would be fair to say that the lieutenant had been over-eager to support his colonel, and to persuade himself that the parade he recalled was the vital parade that Crawley was accused by Smales of failing to attend.

The court, however, rejected Smales' protest. They found Lieutenant Bennitt's explanation 'perfectly satisfactory' and that owing to the long time that had elapsed he had mistaken the parade on 30 April for that on 1 May. The fact that, if Smales had not known of Bennitt's true whereabouts, his evidence would have been damning so far as Smales was concerned, did not, apparently, call for any kind of censure.

Smales, in opening his defence, claimed that Lieutenant Bennitt had 'attempted to hoodwink the court, to cover his untruthfulness, by describing the muster parade and dismounted watering parade as so much alike that he had taken one for the other. It so happens, however, that there is no sort of similarity between the two, beyond the fact of there being on both parades both men and horses.'

But this only produced a formal expression of disapproval by the court of the 'impeachment of the truthfulness and honour of Lieutenant Bennitt whose explanation is still considered by the court to be perfectly satisfactory'.

Colonel Crawley called other officers who gave evidence about his presence on the disputed parades, or how they interpreted his remarks about duelling and his general manner of speech and behaviour towards his officers. It appeared that he was not actually on the parade, but was about the horse lines. Whether he could, even technically, describe himself as being on parade may be doubted. However, according to his witnesses, he 'was around', as might be said, on the days in question.

Much of the evidence was of a negative nature: officers had never heard the colonel express himself in 'coarse, vulgar or ungentlemanlike language towards any officer of the regiment'.

The picture that emerged from the colonel's witnesses was of a man who was a strict disciplinarian: severe on duty, but not so off duty; and in this respect it is fair to say that the picture may not have been an inaccurate one.

5

The colonel's move

CAPTAIN SMALES, in presenting his defence, made it quite clear to begin with that the monthly muster parade was a compulsory one at which the men and horses were checked, and it was obligatory for the commanding officer to be present. This had been acknowledged in cross-examination by Colonel Crawley. But what was meant by 'present'?

Crawley had claimed that during the parade of 1 January 1862 he was actually in the men's rooms inspecting them and 'looking after the comfort of the troops' and that the troop sergeant-majors had been ordered to be present for this purpose in the barracks. Nevertheless, Crawley considered he was present at the parade also 'in the sense in which it is meant by the regulations'.

But it is to be doubted whether the regulations meant anything else by the words 'on parade' than being literally on parade.

Captain Smales outlined in his opening speech the evidence he intended to call. It appeared to be formidable. He told the court:

'I will prove that the prosecutor's statement of looking after the comfort of the troops, arranging barrack furniture etc., assisted by the quartermaster and troop sergeant-majors . . . is another statement utterly at variance with fact, for I will produce the quartermaster himself, and the troop sergeant-majors before this court, who will state upon oath that they were every one of them present on the muster parade on 1 January 1862 and were mustered by me.'

Smales also revealed that he would call evidence that officers waited in the barrack rooms for half an hour *after* the muster parade until Colonel Crawley arrived, making his first appearance of the day 'not much, if at all, before eight o'clock'. The parade had been at 6.30 a.m.

Incredible though it may appear, Colonel Crawley's soldier-servant, Private Walsh, had already been at work, threatening one of Smales' principal witnesses, Paymaster Sergeant G. W. Bennett.

The colonel's batman, when it became known that Bennett would give evidence, warned Mrs Bennett that they were 'a ruined family' if the paymaster sergeant gave evidence for the defence of Captain Smales.

But Bennett, 'a most trustworthy N.C.O.' according to Smales, refused to be intimidated. He gave his evidence on 21 April 1862, the first day of the defence. He was the second witness, and the first actually to confirm Captain Smales' allegations against the colonel.

Captain Smales asked him:

'Who commanded the monthly muster parade on 1 May 1861?'

'Captain Weir.'

'Who commanded the monthly muster parade on 1 June 1861?'

'Captain Weir.'

'Who commanded the monthly muster parade on 1 January 1862?'

'Major Thesiger.'

'Was Lieutenant-Colonel Crawley present on the monthly muster parade on 1 May 1861 at any time during which the officers, non-commissioned officers, rank and file, troop horses and officers' chargers were being mustered?'

'No, he was not.'

'Was Lieutenant-Colonel Crawley present on the monthly muster parade on 1 June 1861 at any time during which the officers, non-commissioned officers, rank and file, troop horses and officers' chargers were being mustered by me?'

'No, he was not.'

The same four-word reply came to the same question about the muster parade of 1 January 1862.

'Is it possible that the officer commanding the monthly muster parade could be on the parade, and you not know he was there?'

'No, it is quite impossible, as I always accompany the paymaster on the parade, and therefore hear him ask the permission of the commanding officer to proceed with the muster and, on the termination of the parade, hear him report to the commanding officer of the parade.'

'Between 1 May 1861 and 1 January 1862 can you positively state how many monthly musters Lieutenant-Colonel Crawley has attended?'

'I could not swear that he had attended more than two—the monthly muster for October, taken on 1 November, and the monthly muster for November taken on 1 December.'

'Between 1 May 1861 and 1 January 1862 inclusive, has Lieutenant-Colonel Crawley's presence, or absence from, the monthly muster parade been the exception?'

'His presence.'

'Have you heard me remark on Lieutenant-Colonel Crawley's absence from the monthly muster parade?'

'I have, frequently.'

'Are you aware that I noted Lieutenant-Colonel Crawley's repeated absence from the monthly muster parade, and that I officially reported such absence to the War Department?'

'I am quite aware of it.'

This was confidently given, positive evidence.

It would be charitable to believe that the attempt by the colonel's batman to intimidate Sergeant Bennett had been made without the colonel's knowledge. But in view of what happened to the sergeant soon after he gave this evidence the kinder thought is difficult to sustain; it must be said, however, that Colonel Crawley later denied having any knowledge of his servant's activities.

Nevertheless, within hours of giving his evidence Sergeant Bennett was, by command of the colonel, ordered from his quarters in the pay office and sent with his family to what Smales described as 'a miserable quarter in the barracks, unsuited in any way to his rank and position in the regiment'.

It was the practice for the paymaster sergeant to be quartered in the pay office building for security reasons and for the proper guarding of the paymaster's books and documents.

Within a few days of the sergeant's removal the pay office

was broken into at night and many confidential books and papers were stolen.

It is difficult not to accept Smales' comment on this incident to the court:

'The paymaster sergeant, without a crime against him, without a shadow of proof of culpability, was instantly placed in arrest, where he remained until the 18th instant [18 May 1862]. This then, is the first realisation of the threat from the prosecutor's servant, "you are a ruined family".'

Among Smales' other witnesses who were to testify to the colonel's absence from parade were the regimental sergeant-major, Mr John Lilley, and other senior N.C.O.s: the adjutant, Lieutenant Fitzsimon was also being called.

To suppose that the R.S.M. and adjutant of a regiment might not know whether or not their commanding officer was present at a parade would be ridiculous. These men were, therefore, extremely dangerous from Colonel Crawley's point of view.

He dealt with this danger to his case by adopting what a contemporary writer called 'extreme measures in order to neutralise their evidence'.

For some days now Colonel Crawley had apparently been investigating the activities of the R.S.M. and other defence witnesses, and his enquiries had not been in vain.

How it came about that one of the troop sergeant-majors decided to make statements to the colonel is not known, but make them he did.

Troop Sergeant-Major Moreton told the colonel that on 4 April at the end of the fourth day's proceedings of the court martial, R.S.M. Lilley had told him to come to his quarters in the evening as he (Lilley) had an account of the first three days of the trial and was going to read it out.

The trial, at this moment, had not had time to get into the local newspapers, although it was, of course, being reported and would be followed eagerly by all English-speaking people in India. So an account of what had so far taken place was naturally of great interest within the regiment.

T.S.M. Moreton duly went to the R.S.M.'s bungalow and there, in a conspiratorial atmosphere, with windows and doors shut, Lilley read out the proceedings. There seems little doubt that Captain Smales, or someone close to him, had passed on this account of the trial. Troop Sergeant-Majors Cotton and McNamara and Sergeant Bernard were other interested members of the little audience.

Moreton seems to have reported the meeting to the colonel without delay and it is reasonable to infer that he was told to 'play along' with the other sergeants and find out as much as he could.

Before the weekend was out he had more to report. In his statement to the colonel he said: 'On Sunday evening, 6 April 1862, about 9.30 I was under the verandah of D Troop talking to Sergeant-Major Wakefield and Sergeant Bernard. About a quarter of an hour previous to this they were told, in my presence, by Sergeant-Major Lilley that the commanding officer had heard that we had seen the proceedings of the court; he also said that the old fellow, meaning the paymaster, felt very much annoyed at the colonel having heard of it. Sergeant-Major Lilley then went away and the following remarks were made by Troop Sergeant-Major Wakefield: "By God, the man who gave the information I will poison him, or in some way make away with him, for he is not fit to live."

'Sergeant Bernard said he thought it was Sergeant-Major McNamara who gave information to the commanding officer, through the orderly-room clerk, Sergeant Reynolds. They both swore they would swear, were they called before the court martial, that they had never seen the proceedings at all.'

Whether the sergeant-majors actually spoke in such moderate and stilted phrases is to be doubted, but the meaning and intention are clear enough.

Colonel Crawley naturally passed on this information to the court and as soon as it reassembled on Monday, 7 April the president announced:

'The proceedings of the first three days have been furnished to the sergeant-major of the 6th Dragoons, and publicly read at his quarters to other non-commissioned officers of the regiment. I consider this highly improper and irregular on the part of the non-commissioned officers and, without accusing anyone in particular of furnishing the proceedings, I hereby forbid anyone attending this court making the proceedings public until the case is closed, as it must be obvious that such an extraordinary proceeding can only be intended to bias the minds of the witnesses on one side or the other, and thus prejudice the matter under investigation.'

Having issued this warning the court dismissed another of Captain Smales' many objections to the way the trial was being conducted, and military justice returned to its curious pursuit of truth.

The following day, when the adjutant, Lieutenant Fitzsimon, was giving evidence for the prosecution (he was a witness on both sides), Smales requested permission to ask him during cross-examination whether Colonel Crawley had not read to him, the adjutant, some of the court proceedings.

The court apparently considered that while it was wrong for Smales' witnesses to read the proceedings in advance of newspaper publication, the same ruling did not apply to one of Colonel Crawley's witnesses—for it disallowed this question on the ground that it was irrelevant.

On 26 April, a Saturday, the fourteenth day of the trial and sixth day of the defence, when already considerable evidence from officers in support of Captain Smales had been given, Colonel Crawley made his move that was to end in tragedy.

Two days earlier he had received a report from his spy among the sergeant-majors, Troop Sergeant-Major Moreton. This was to the effect that Troop Sergeant-Major Wakefield had told him on the previous Sunday that a copy of Captain Smales' opening speech for the defence was available, and that it had been handed to Moreton by R.S.M. Lilley late that night. Moreton made a copy of it and passed this on to Colonel Crawley with his report.

Moreton's final report referred to Wednesday, 23 April: 'about 9.30 p.m. I was sent for by R.S.M. Lilley on matters of duty, when the following expressions were made use of by R.S.M. Lilley in the presence of T.S.M. Wakefield, T.S.M. Duval and myself. "By God, if that **** down there [pointing towards Colonel Crawley's bungalow and meaning Colonel Crawley] cross-questions me on anything I will let out about his carrying on, and how he has often made me shed tears; by God, I will pitch it into him stiff enough." '

Delicacy apparently forbade recording of the actual epithet applied to the colonel, but its uncomplimentary nature is clear enough.

Having pondered on this report for a day or so the colonel acted on the Saturday by summoning separately to his quarters Lilley, Duval, Wakefield and Moreton.

Undoubtedly he simply interviewed Moreton so that suspicion of his spying should not fall upon him.

The interviews, for the other three men, were nerve-testing experiences. The adjutant was not present and the colonel's harsh, parade-ground manner and short temper were given full range.

He accused each of them of clandestinely reading the proceedings of the court, and of being party to threatening words against himself.

His tactics with Wakefield were somewhat intimidating: he picked up a ruler from his desk, tapped him on the chest with it, and said: 'You have more in your breast about this than any other man, and I'll have it out.' He threatened to put Wakefield in irons if he did not tell all he knew about what the colonel called 'the cabal' against him.

He used similar methods against each of the sergeant-majors in turn, his manner and the general gravity of the examination being enhanced by the presence of two other officers—both witnesses for the prosecution in the Smales case.

All three men made statements admitting to some extent the truth of what Moreton had reported; and, of course, none of them knew what the others had said.

On the strength of their admissions Colonel Crawley charged them with conspiracy and reported his action to the Mhow divisional commander, Major-General Farrell, who ordered that they be kept in close arrest pending further instructions. The mere suggestion of organised insubordination was enough to provoke the severest reaction in view of memories of the recent Indian Mutiny.

Lilley learned of his close confinement about 8 p.m. on the day of his interrogation. He was sitting on the front verandah of his bungalow with his wife, enjoying, no doubt, the cooler evening air. The Eastern night would have been aquiver with the chant of crickets, and perhaps a horse whinnied or shook its halter over the lines; the familiar sounds of a cavalry camp when night has fallen.

Along the line of terraced bungalows, of which Lilley's was the corner one, came the clump of marching feet. Three men and a sergeant were approaching through the darkness. It was difficult for the Lilleys to see who it was with only the faint glow from the oil lamp in their bungalow behind them.

There was a shout of 'Halt' and the sudden crunch of stamping feet in the dusty camp road; then silence.

The sergeant-major stood up and walked to the edge of the verandah.

'Who's there?' he called.

'It's S'arn Faulds, S'arn-Major. Sorry, but I have orders to put a sentry on you.'

'Whose orders?' Lilley's voice rose angrily.

'Colonel Crawley's.'

'Am I to have no communication with my wife?'

'There was nothing said about that, S'arn-Major. Just to watch you.'

Private Robert McVey was detached from the little group as the first sentry. His orders were not to allow anyone except the surgeon to speak or write to the sergeant-major. The sergeant-major's native servant was to be searched whenever he entered or left the bungalow in case he carried a message to or from anyone.

Another sharp command, and Sergeant Faulds marched off his remaining two sentries to post them over the two troop sergeant-majors, Duval and Wakefield.

And so began the ritual of close arrest: two hours on and four off for the sentries. A different face every two hours, a different pair of eyes to watch Lilley.

On 28 April Major-General Farrell wrote to the Commander-in-Chief, Bombay, Lieutenant-General Sir William Mansfield, and asked for his decision as to how the sergeant-majors should be dealt with.

But, for the moment, we will return to the courtroom where, on this same day, Monday, 28 April, the trial of Captain Smales resumed after the Sunday adjournment.

Captain Smales immediately protested that Colonel Crawley had placed three of his witnesses in close arrest, with sentries over them—'Three of the most respectable non-commissioned officers in the regiment.'

Smales asked for the protection of the court on the ground that 'If such proceedings go on, before I have come to the close of my defence I will have no witnesses to produce.'

Smales assured the court that he had not disobeyed the instructions about publishing the evidence given.

This was less than frank: it may be that Smales had not passed on any proceedings of the court, but he had handed over a copy of what his defence speech was to be. Thus he could say he had obeyed the court's ruling because what he had made available to the sergeant-majors was evidence still to be given to the court.

Troop Sergeant-Major Moreton, in his role of *agent provocateur*, reported in his statement to Crawley that he said to Sergeant-Major Wakefield: 'It is a wonder the paymaster gave you the papers after what happened about the last [meaning the remarks of the President of the Court Martial on account of the first three days' proceedings being read out to the sergeant-majors] and Sergeant-Major Wakefield replied: "Oh, he doesn't care a damn now that the proceedings are allowed to be published." ' Wakefield meant publication in the local newspapers.

But whatever knowledge Captain Smales may or may not have had about how his defence came to be in the hands of the sergeant-majors, his plea against the arrest of his witnesses achieved little.

The court considered his protest and decided that it was unable to deal with the question of the arrests; but it ruled that the three witnesses could still give their evidence.

Captain Smales resumed the heavy burden of his defence.

6

Ordeal of R.S.M. Lilley

COLONEL CRAWLEY had overlooked one thing when he questioned the sergeant-majors. He did not warn them that anything they said might be used as evidence. This lack of the essential ingredient in legally examining suspects ought to have led to the prompt release of the three men: but it did not.

On 6 May 1862 Lieutenant-General Sir William Mansfield wrote to Major-General Farrell to the effect that the evidence against the sergeant-majors would not support a charge of conspiracy because the necessary warning had not been given.

Nevertheless, he considered R.S.M. Lilley was totally unsuited for his position and ought to be removed from it. Meanwhile, instead of ordering the men's release—there being no evidence on which to bring a charge against them—he instructed Farrell that they should be kept in close arrest until the conclusion of Captain Smales' trial.

The reasons he gave for this irregular order were (1) that they had narrowly escaped committing a most serious crime and ought to be kept from the temptation of repeating it; (2) that they should be kept safe from being 'tampered with to concoct their evidence'; (3) that the charge brought against them by Colonel Crawley ought not to appear to be condoned by their release until the whole of the evidence had been heard—in case more evidence against them came out during the trial.

Sir William Mansfield said, after the dreadful consequences of his order had horrified England, that he had been under the impression the court martial would end about the same time as his orders reached Mhow, and that the sergeant-majors would therefore have been released almost immediately. Perhaps he had been: perhaps no such thought ever entered his head—until tragedy produced the need for it.

In fact, owing to the indisposition of Captain Smales, the trial dragged on until 7 June 1862. Thus, instead of being in close arrest for a few days the men were subjected to close confinement—without being charged with anything—for weeks.

The adjutant, Lieutenant Fitzsimon, a friend of Smales, was somewhat sympathetic towards Sergeant-Major Lilley, and did not inspect for himself the exact place where the sentries were posted, although he passed on the colonel's orders regarding close arrest to the acting R.S.M. Mr Cotton.

Cotton, being a friend of Lilley, may, in the beginning, have turned a blind eye as to where the sentries carried out their duties. At first they were outside the bungalow; then Colonel Crawley noticed that they were in the sun and instructed that they stand beneath the Lilley's porch. He did not, at this time, object to the sentries being outside the house.

Shortly afterwards orders were given for the sentries to be posted inside the bungalow.

Within a few days a corporal of the guard was tried by regimental court martial on Colonel Crawley's orders for 'neglect of duty in posting a sentry at the door, instead of within the house occupied by R.S.M. Lilley' and was sentenced to forty-two days' imprisonment and reduced in rank.

There was a stormy scene in Crawley's office when he gave the adjutant a dressing-down for not knowing what close arrest meant. It meant more than posting a sentry outside a man's house, said Crawley, it meant that a sentry kept his prisoner in sight day and night and to do that he would have to be posted inside the house.

Sergeant-Major Cotton pointed out that Lilley was a married man and that his wife was ill, requiring his attention. He had to rub embrocation on her chest daily.

The colonel flew into a rage at this temporising with his order.

'Officer or soldier, married or single, I don't care a damn, the duty shall be done. See to it, Sergeant-major.'

There was no room for argument: the sentries received strict instructions that from then on they were to observe Lilley from inside his bungalow.

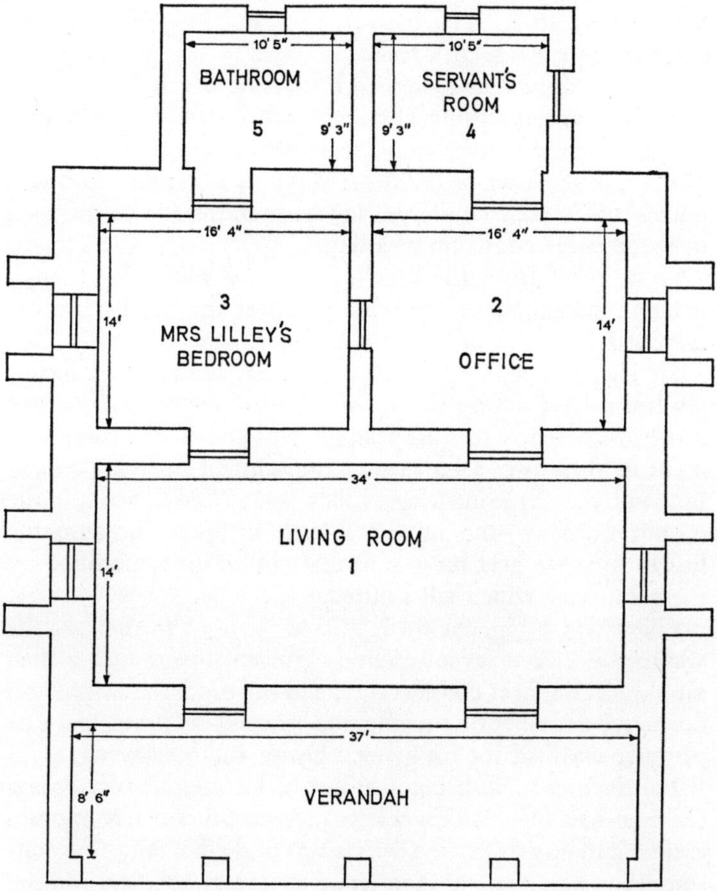

The first quarters

The regimental sergeant-major's quarters were to become the centre of horrified public interest throughout India and Britain as the story unfolded, and they must be briefly described.

His normal bungalow home—the first place of confinement—had five rooms and a verandah some 37 ft. wide. Behind the verandah was the living room, a spacious 34 ft. across the full width of the bungalow, and 14 ft. deep. Behind the living room were two bedrooms each 16 ft. 4 in. by 14 ft. (one of which Lilley used as an office), and behind them two small rooms each 10 ft. 5 in. by 9 ft. 3 in., one being a bathroom and the other a servant's room.

The bungalow had an arched brick roof which was covered with straw as some protection against the searing summer sun.

These quarters were quite spacious compared with some N.C.O. bungalows of the time. But it is one thing to lead a normal life in such a building, and quite another to be confined to it for twenty-four hours a day.

Some relief from the heat indoors was gained by Lilley's hanging wet mats at the windows; but the rooms became oppressively hot at this time of the year.

Sir Hugh Rose, Commander-in-Chief, India, and a distinguished soldier during the Indian Mutiny, wrote: 'Indian heat is the great enemy to European life and health. . . . Imprisonment is, therefore, a far greater punishment in India than in England. . . . Sergeant-Major Lilley was placed in arrest in the month of May—the hottest month in India, because the Indian summer heat has not at that period been modified by the great rains which fall a little later. . . .'

Lilley was a big, fat man, just on 5 ft. 11 in. tall and he weighed between seventeen and eighteen stones: such a man would feel the heat considerably, and the sudden change from the active daily life of a regimental sergeant-major to that of a prisoner was bad for his general health and well-being.

Bereavement had become a part of his life: his two young children had died within weeks of each other a few months earlier, and now his wife Clarissa was in the last stages of consumption. She was suffering from dysentery and the racking pain of ravaged lungs. She required almost constant nursing, although her condition varied from day to day. Sometimes she could get up and go about the camp; on other days she could sit up in the house, and on other days she had to remain in bed.

What she really needed in her condition was the attention and comfort of another woman. But by order of Colonel Crawley, because of the possibility of R.S.M. Lilley communicating with others, no women were allowed in the bungalow.

Mrs Lilley had for some time resisted the advice of the regimental doctor that she should go into hospital. She knew

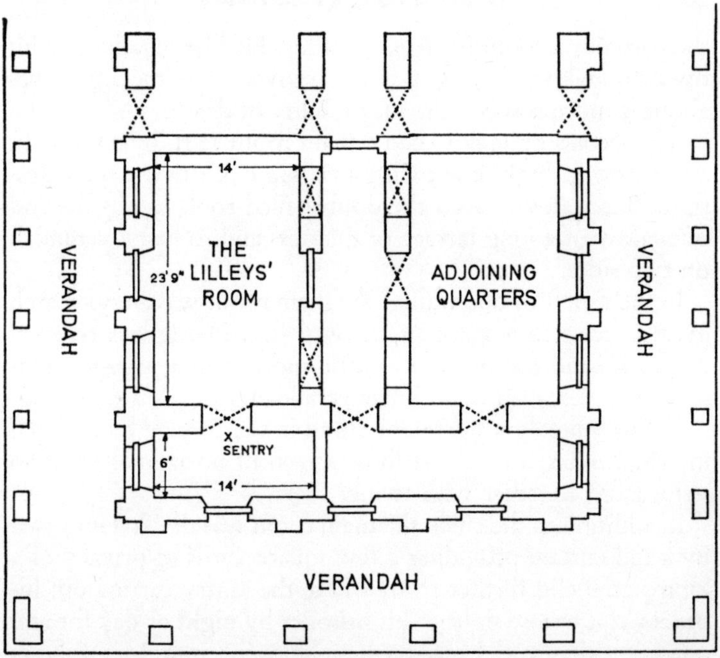

The second quarters

she had not long to live and was determined to pass what little time remained to her in her own home.

It was therefore necessary for her husband to nurse and wait upon her and perform all those offices which under different circumstances she would have received from a woman friend.

Confinement in this bungalow lasted sixteen days. Then the Lilleys were transferred to what was virtually a one-room bungalow. The reason for the move had nothing to do with Colonel Crawley (although he was blamed for it), and he was not satisfied with the accommodation to which the couple were moved.

The move had to take place because an extensive programme of rebuilding the barracks was going on at Mhow, and the camp engineer had requested that the Lilley bungalow be vacated for demolition.

In spite of some efforts by Colonel Crawley to find better alternative accommodation there was none available.

It was just one more fateful piece falling into place; part of the pattern of doom for R.S.M. Lilley. Had he remained in his own bungalow he might have survived; but the move has about it, in retrospect, the inevitability of death.

The second bungalow had a main room 14 ft. by 23 ft. 9 in. and was 9 ft. high, lined with a ceiling cloth to catch the dust that filtered down from the double-tiled roof. It was the end bungalow of a long terrace of quarters and so had a verandah on two sides.

In the centre of one wall of the main room was an open arch giving access to a space 14 ft. by 6 ft. wide. It was referred to as a second room but was little more than a passage or, as some people called it, an inner verandah.

In this bungalow the sentry stood in the passage by the arch in which hung a chick—a loose screen of horizontal bamboo strips laced together with twine.

In addition to the chick the main room was divided into two by a red curtain providing a few square yards of privacy of a kind at the end further from where the sentry carried out his orders 'not to lose sight of his prisoner by night or day for any purpose whatever' except when he went into Mrs Lilley's room. The sentries had orders not to follow him there.

But the existence of the curtain only served to hamper what flow of air there was and added to the stifling atmosphere where 'was done all that nature entails on humanity'.

The appalling conditions under which the dying woman and her husband spent their last days together perhaps require no further description.

Conversation had to be carried on in an undertone to avoid the sentry's hearing what passed between husband and wife, or what the doctor said during his visits.

On 7 May, while still imprisoned in the first bungalow, Lilley began his evidence for the defence.

Captain Smales took him through his damaging testimony against Colonel Crawley, evidence which confirmed the truth of the allegations Smales had made in the letter that led to his court martial.

Lilley testified that he had seen the colonel on only two muster parades between 1 May 1861 and 1 January 1862.

'If Lieutenant-Colonel Crawley was present I should know it,' he said.

The sergeant-major told of the colonel's unusually harsh manner towards his subordinates, commissioned and non-commissioned. It was evident that the colonel was a man of powerful and rasping voice, and of intimidating manner. Lilley admitted having been brought to tears by the colonel on one occasion.

None of these attributes in an officer are, of course, unknown in the services even today, and their display is the only way in which some men can assert their authority and maintain what they conceive to be discipline. They are not the best of officers, but their manner is not an offence known to military law, unless it be carried to extreme.

It was Smales' original complaint that Crawley's manner in this respect *was* extreme.

Smales now turned to Lilley's character and military background, which were important in view of Crawley's allegations both now and on a later occasion.

'How long have you been in the 6th Dragoons, and how long have you been regimental sergeant-major?'

'I have served in the 6th Dragoons eighteen years and about five months,' replied Lilley, 'and I shall have been regimental sergeant-major seven years next 3 July, to the best of my belief.'

'Were you recommended by Colonel Shute and Lieutenant-Colonel Fitzwygram for the adjutancy of the regiment?'

'In Kirkee—I don't remember the date—Colonel Shute told me he had recommended me for the adjutancy of the regiment, and said he was very sorry but he had received an answer that it could not be given in the regiment at the time: but I was noted to the Horse Guards when an opportunity would offer.'

'Have you ever been under an arrest before, since you have been regimental sergeant-major?'

'No.'

'State to the court, as near as you can, the last act harsh and unusual of the prosecutor's towards you.'

'The last act was the present occasion, by a sentry being placed at my bedroom door, where my sick wife is lying. The door is quite open, and the sentry is posted about two feet from my bed.'

The court apparently saw nothing in this fact to call for comment, and presumably neither did it excite compassion.

Colonel Crawley made enquiries later that day as to the exact position of the sentries in relation to Mrs Lilley's bed and had them moved to a different part of the house further away from her bedroom door.

But, for the moment, in court, the colonel was more concerned with the dangerous nature of the sergeant-major's evidence in relation to the prosecution.

He at once interrupted as Lilley made his complaint, and said:

'Mr President and gentlemen: with your permission I wish to put a question to this witness on a matter which is not immediately before the court, but which it is absolutely necessary for me to put with regard to his credibility, as I have reason to believe he has been tampered with. I wish to ask with reference to the orders of the President of the Court Martial directing that the proceedings of the court shall not be divulged till the conclusion of the trial.'

Although, of course, it was open to the colonel to cross-examine the R.S.M. and try to prove by it that his evidence might not be reliable, it was highly improper to suggest, as his personal opinion, that he believed Lilley had been 'tampered with'.

But the court seemed to see nothing wrong in it and allowed the colonel to question Lilley along the lines he had indicated.

'Have you,' Colonel Crawley asked, 'at any time seen and read a copy of the prisoner's defence, either before or after it was delivered by him to the court, and prior to its publication here at Mhow in the Poona or Bombay newspapers? If you have seen or read it, when and where did you see or read it?'

'I have seen a copy of the prisoner's defence. I read it over in my house. I don't recollect the date exactly, but I believe it was on a Sunday evening, and it was the day before it was read out in court. No one was with me at the time.'

'From whom did you receive a copy of the defence?'

'From Troop Sergeant-Major Wakefield.'

'Do you know why the defence was sent to you, and did you receive any message about it at the time?'

'I have no idea why it was sent to me, and I did not receive any message at the time. When I received it from Sergeant-Major Wakefield he told me to give it to another sergeant-major. I don't recollect who it was. I did not know the handwriting of the papers, and I never saw them any more after that.'

'Can you swear who sent you a copy of the defence?'

'I have already stated that I received it from Sergeant-Major Wakefield.'

'Did you, at any time on that day, communicate the contents of the defence to anyone else?'

'Not that I am aware of.'

'Have you, or not, stated to Lieutenant-Colonel Crawley that you received the defence from a native?'

'I did say so, but since then I believe that I did not.'

'Were you not aware that this court had forbidden the publication, in the lines, of the proceedings, as it tended to bias the evidence, especially when done in such a marked manner, through you?'

'I think I was. I had read the remarks of the court that had previously been made.'

Lilley's evidence ended at this point and he left the court.

Lilley appears to have been slightly evasive in manner. He had obviously lied to Crawley during his earlier interrogation with a view to shielding Wakefield, and although he now gave Wakefield's name under oath he, ironically, withheld the name of Sergeant-Major Moreton, the informer, to whom he passed the papers from Captain Smales.

It is also to be doubted whether the regimental sergeant-major would not recognise the handwriting of the paymaster.

Captain Smales naturally objected to Colonel Crawley's attack on one of his principal witnesses, and lodged a formal protest.

It will be remembered that Smales had been denied the opportunity of cross-examining the adjutant, Lieutenant Fitzsimon, about publicising the court proceedings. He recalled the circumstances to the court:

'The prosecutor states he "has reason to believe this witness has been tampered with". To support this assumption the court have permitted the prosecutor to put a question to the witness of a directly similar character and tendency which the court refused to allow me to do to Lieutenant and Adjutant Fitzsimon.

'When Lieutenant Fitzsimon was under examination I put a question as to whether the prosecutor had not read some days' proceedings to the witness. The question was rejected by the court as irrelevant.

'Again, the prosecutor himself employed as an amanuensis—for many days after he had been warned to give evidence—one of my witnesses. Thus the prosecutor himself has given the greatest publicity to the proceedings of the court, and now attempts to impugn one of my witnesses upon merely hearsay evidence.'

Smales also protested that the suggestion that Lilley had 'been tampered with' was an unjustified slur on him, Smales, because of the obvious inference that he had done the tampering.

Smales went on to claim on various legal grounds his right to examine the colonel.

The blatant unfairness of Smales' position on this point, at least, must have become evident even to the judicially myopic panel before whom he appeared, for they agreed that the questioning of the adjutant, previously refused, should now be permitted; and they also gave permission for Smales to examine the colonel.

The adjutant was recalled and testified that several days' court proceedings had, in fact, been read to him by Colonel Crawley.

And so the dismal parody of a trial dragged on: its proceedings in transcript comprise well over 120,000 words. It is a story of petty quarrels, bickering, and abuse of military position and power—and a man had to die for it.

However, an outline of the more relevant issues is necessary to understand the eventual court martial of Lieutenant-Colonel Crawley himself.

The two sergeant-majors arrested with Lilley both testified

that Colonel Crawley was not on the parades mentioned in Captain Smales' insubordinate letter. But Smales was not allowed to question either man on the subject of his arrest and confinement during the court martial.

Altogether twenty-three witnesses supported Captain Smales' case and the evidence for the defence, taken as a whole, proved that Smales' allegations about the colonel's absences from parade and his general conduct towards his officers were true.

His allegations were clearly not 'false and malicious' as described in the charges against him, although, by its nature, Captain Smales' letter of complaint was no doubt insubordinate.

But there is an enormous difference between writing an insubordinate letter and inventing damaging accusations against a superior officer.

Here was the difficulty, the charges being framed as they were: if Smales were acquitted then Crawley would at the same time be branded as unfit to hold his position. Smales' allegations *had* to be found false to save Crawley.

Smales' examination of Crawley also aided his defence, if there had been anyone listening with justice in mind.

'Has the manner in which I have conducted my official duties as paymaster of the 6th Dragoons, since I have been under your command, met with your approval, or has it been such as to cause you to make any complaint of such official conduct to higher authority?' Smales asked.

The colonel replied: 'Paymaster Smales, in his official capacity as paymaster of the 6th Dragoons, has conducted the routine duties of his office, as far as they concern myself personally, without giving me offence or annoyance. I cannot say the same as regards other officers, for I have had complaints from more than one of the manner in which they have been treated by Paymaster Smales, when they have had occasion to go to his office to draw pay.

'Complaints have been made to me by certain officers of having to suffer the indignity of waiting with a clerk in the office until it suited the prisoner's convenience to pay them. These complaints were not brought before me in an official form and therefore I did not consider it necessary to send them on to higher authority.'

'Be so good as to state to the court from whom you have had complaints,' said Smales.

'I have had complaints from an officer who has left the regiment, Captain Gordon; and also from one who is now present with it, Captain Renshaw.'

Of Captain Gordon, who flickers momentarily into the trial by name only, and is gone, nothing is known. But Captain Renshaw was the officer whose wife had so outraged the feelings of the married officers and their wives.

Renshaw was naturally prominent among the Crawleyites —those who supported the colonel's liberal attitude on the 'social and moral' question. So Renshaw would be at loggerheads with Smales, the leader of the anti-Crawley faction—and would take offence on the slightest pretext, and possibly make such complaint about him to the colonel as opportunity offered.

'Was not the social and moral question, already referred to in evidence before this court, the very first source of misunderstanding that ever took place between you and myself?'

The colonel's answer was revealing, and the court was soon to take steps to prevent Smales' developing the implication of the reply.

'I believe it was,' said Crawley. 'I have no recollection of any other previously. So far from having misunderstanding with Paymaster Smales, I had on every occasion previous to that question being raised given to the paymaster every support in my power in the discharge of his duties as paymaster. So far as I am aware, I have done so since in the discharge of his official duties.'

'As you find no fault with my official conduct, for what reason did you place me in your confidential report which you submitted at the last inspection of General Hale at Ahmednugger? Was it upon the social question?'

This was obviously a difficult question for the colonel in view of his earlier reply, and he could only have admitted that his attitude towards Smales had been influenced by personal animus arising out of their conflict over Mrs Renshaw.

However, he was not troubled to find an answer because the court decided that this was a question which ought not to be put.

Captain Smales turned—with resignation it may be assumed—to other matters.

'On the 22nd day's proceedings of the court you recorded, by permission of the court, a protest to the effect that you had reason to believe that certain defence witnesses had been tampered with. Be so good as to state to the court the party by whom you had reason to believe these witnesses had been tampered with.'

'From the statements of these witnesses themselves, taken down myself in the presence of three officers of the regiment, I have reason to believe that they were tampered with by Captain Smales or his agents,' replied the colonel.

'Were the statements you procured from Troop Sergeant-Major Wakefield, or others, voluntary statements, or were any threatened to be placed in irons if they did not state all they knew on the subject alluded to?'

This question, although it embodied the great bulwark of all good evidence—that it should not have been extracted under duress—was overruled by the court on the ground that it was 'foreign to the charge'.

But the very fact that Smales was armed with such information with which to cross-examine proved that he had been in touch with Lilley or the other sergeant-majors since their close confinement, which began almost immediately after the interrogation by Crawley.

It is a fact, not known at the time but established much later, that Captain Smales had been writing almost daily to one of the arrested men, and notes had been slipped to him through a hole in the wall by a sergeant whose quarters were next door.

Thus Captain Smales' assertion that he had not been communicating with the sergeant-majors was not true, and his challenge to Colonel Crawley as to whom he thought had been 'tampering' with the arrested men was simply a bluff.

Smales now tried to probe the colonel in another weak spot.

'Has it been reported to you in any way that your soldier servant, Private Walsh, 6th Dragoons, has been endeavouring to tamper with or intimidate certain witnesses for the defence, or persons likely to become witnesses?'

The court considered this question and again ruled that it could not be put as it would only bring forward hearsay evidence: 'but the prisoner is at liberty to bring forward evidence of any person who may have been tampered with, or intimidated.'

By this time, of course, Sergeant Bennett, the paymaster's assistant, had already been removed from his comfortable quarters and rehoused in less pleasant conditions for his temerity in giving evidence for Captain Smales. And he was already under arrest on a charge arising out of the loss of official papers stolen out of the quarters from which he had been removed—a proceeding that seems a little unreasonable to say the least.

But Captain Smales did not call Bennett again. Perhaps he considered it futile to recall the sergeant and add to the man's difficulties. It was also extremely unlikely that the court would have listened to any such evidence tending to expose the true enmity of Colonel Crawley towards Smales and his supporters.

It was now Saturday, 10 May 1862. Smales had no more witnesses to call and he was granted a week's recess in which to prepare his concluding statement for the defence. But he was unwell the following Saturday and the court was further adjourned until 19 May. It happened that Colonel Crawley was unable to attend on this day and so the court did not re-assemble until Saturday, 24 May.

Smales concluded his defence with a long speech reviewing the evidence and maintaining that he had proved the statements made in his letter to be true.

Meanwhile, the three sergeant-majors had continued throughout all this time to be confined to their quarters, and allowed out only for a limited amount of exercise—two hours a day—requested by the medical officer.

7

Death of a sergeant-major

REGIMENTAL SERGEANT-MAJOR John Lilley died unpleasantly in an apoplectic fit in the early hours of 25 May 1862. He was thirty-seven.

From statements made by sentries it is possible to reconstruct part of his last day of life.

That his death came partly as a result of being imprisoned in the second small bungalow, together with the attendant worry of his wife's condition and his own position, there was no doubt. What was never entirely resolved satisfactorily was how much his apoplexy might have been due to drinking spirits during his confinement, how much he drank, and whether he was accustomed to taking strong drink regularly or not.

We can join him and his wife on the verandah of their last home at 8 p.m. on 23 May, when Lance-Corporal Fred Holman came on as the sentry from 8–10 p.m.

Mrs Lilley was sitting in a cane lounging chair and her husband was lying on a couch which had been brought out from the main room.

Lance-Corporal Holman began to walk up and down the verandah, possibly reluctant to stand and stare at his R.S.M. and his wife to the embarrassment of them all.

'Don't walk about, sentry,' said Lilley after about ten minutes of it, 'I want to get to sleep.'

Holman took up an unobtrusive position and remained still. The minutes passed in silence until, at 8.30, the drummer of the guard marched briskly to the corner of H Troop quarters, a few feet from where Lilley lay, and rattled out the defaulters' call. Lilley awoke with a start.

'Damn the boy,' he muttered. 'Who's the sentry?'

'It's Holman, sir.'

'Oh, yes, Holman.' Lilley shrugged off sleep and began to talk. 'I heard today that Bob Davies had asked you to go into the orderly room.'

'Yes, he did,' said Holman. 'But I'm not going. My eyesight isn't good enough for that kind of work.'

Lilley snorted: 'I should think not. You'd never get on with Colonel Crawley.'

There was desultory conversation until 9 p.m. when Lilley groped under his couch and withdrew a long riding boot. From it he took a bottle of brandy. He offered the bottle towards Holman:

'Will you have a drop?'

'No thanks, S'arn-Major. I've got a bilious headache.'

Lilley put the bottle to his own mouth and took a long drink from it.

Mrs Lilley looked up. 'My dear, dear man,' she said, 'don't drink so much at once: it will only do you harm.'

'I can't help it,' said Lilley, 'it's the only thing that solaces me.'

Mrs Lilley remained on the verandah until 9.50 p.m. and then went inside to her bed. The sergeant-major stayed where he was but so far as is known did not drink any more brandy up to the time Holman was relieved at ten o'clock.

Another sentry, Private Drabble, also saw Lilley drinking brandy and heard Mrs Lilley ask him to 'knock it off' and come to bed.

Lilley was still on the verandah when Holman came on again at 2 a.m. He said nothing for ten minutes: it was quite dark on the verandah, although there may have been some light from the moon or sky. It was certainly not easy to make out faces plainly even from a few feet away.

Lilley suddenly stirred and swung himself into an upright position on the couch.

'Who's the sentry?' he asked.

'It's Holman again, sir. I've just come on.'

'I'm glad it's you, Holman. Well, I think I'll go in now. Will you have a drink?' He held up the bottle again.

'No thanks, sir.'

Lilley up-ended the bottle at his lips and emptied it. He put the bottle on the floor and asked Holman to help him in with the couch.

'Throw that bottle away will you, Holman, please,' he said as they lifted the couch inside.

The sergeant-major stayed in the bungalow for the rest of Holman's watch, which he kept from the verandah.

At 8 a.m. it was Holman's watch again. R.S.M. Lilley had got the couch out on to the verandah again and was lying on it reading the *Deccan Herald*.

He obviously liked Holman, and was soon talking to him again.

'I feel sick, Holman,' he said. 'I'm full of wind.' He patted his ample stomach. An hour later he was asking Holman to feel his stomach. 'See how hard it is?' he said, as Holman extended a hand to his abdomen and prodded it.

There is no way of knowing how much brandy was in the bottle first mentioned by Lance-Corporal Holman when Lilley took it from the riding boot. All that is known is that there was sufficient for him to take a long pull at it and for Mrs Lilley to notice the fact.

At about 9.30 a.m. Lilley began to complain of severe pain in the stomach. Groaning from time to time, he produced a piece of paper and handed it to Holman.

'Holman, write a note to the apothecary, will you, please. Ask him to send Dr Barnett to see me.'

Holman wrote the note and Lilley's native servant took it. Dr Barnett, the assistant regimental surgeon, arrived at 10 a.m., as Holman was being relieved. Lilley told the doctor of his pain and his distended abdomen. He also complained of a dull pain in his head; and Dr Barnett found 'the surface of the body intensely hot'.

The doctor tried first that panacea of the old-time medico, a heavy dose of castor oil; and hot fomentations were applied to Lilley's abdomen. This treatment did not have much effect, and the next certain thing known about Lilley's last hours comes from Lance-Corporal Holman, in a statement:

'I was posted again at 2 p.m. Sergeant-Major Lilley was in his bungalow. He came out and asked me to escort him to the rear: this was about 2.15 p.m. He still complained of great pain in his stomach. He told me he had drunk twelve bottles of soda water since breakfast. He drank more while I was on sentry that day.

'He asked me a second time to feel his stomach: it was very hard.'

About 3.30 p.m. Holman watched Lilley bathe his head in a tub of cold water for about twenty minutes. Holman was relieved at 4 p.m.

The guard was changed at 6 p.m. and the first sentry on was Private Charles Ewing. Lilley came to the chick as Ewing was being posted in the small room, and showed himself to the new corporal of the guard. He then had his tea and went out to the verandah.

Dr Barnett saw him again shortly afterwards and, the castor oil having had little effect and the abdominal pains continuing, Lilley was given eight grains of calomel, a strong purgative.

He was also prescribed a medicine to relieve the pains: it was a mixture of hyoscyamus, nitric ether and camphor to be taken at bedtime.

At 8 p.m. Ewing was relieved by Private Robert Rutherford, who tells us: 'About 9.30 Sergeant-Major Lilley prepared to go to bed, and washed his feet. He came out to the verandah to a closed stool which was in the corner, and then returned and went to bed. Before going in to bed he took a draught of some high-coloured liquid out of a tumbler, but I do not know what it was, nor did I see him pour it out.'

An inference may have been drawn that this liquid was brandy, and it may well have been. But it is also possible that it was the soothing draught, which would have been light green in colour.

At about 10.15 p.m. came the first real signs that Sergeant-Major Lilley was seriously ill.

He called out loudly for Sergeant-Major Cotton who lived in the end bungalow of the next terrace—next door to the Lilleys.

'What is it?' called Cotton.

'I'm ill.'

A few moments later Sergeant-Major Cotton hurried in.

'What's the matter, John?'

'I'm dying,' said Lilley, a little prematurely as it turned out. 'Get the doctor for me.'

Cotton said a few reassuring words and went to send for Dr Barnett.

The doctor arrived about 11 p.m. and, in his own words, 'a large cathartic enema was then administered which afforded immediate relief to the abdominal uneasiness'.

Dr Barnett stayed about half an hour during which time Lilley lay restless, and moaning a little. The doctor noticed that his eyes were dull and heavy, 'with an anxious expression of countenance'. Cold pads were applied to his head and chest.

The sergeant-major then went to bed again and, according to the sentry on duty between 10 and 12 p.m., Private McVey, he appeared to be easier, 'though I heard him complain of being thirsty and ask his wife for something to drink'.

Mrs Lilley, ill though she was herself, had not gone to bed and was sitting at a table in the half of the curtain-divided room which was used as a day-room, when Private Ewing came on duty again. Lilley was behind the curtain in the bedroom.

About 12.15 a.m. the sergeant-major came through from the bedroom and complained to his wife of wind in the stomach again.

Private Ewing 'saw him take a large decanter which stood on a side-table and pour out half a tumblerful of brandy, and drink it off. He then went back to his bedroom.'

The last macabre hours in the life of John Lilley ticked away. His sick wife drooped over a table by the light of an oil lamp; a sentry a few paces away; and behind the dividing curtain the doomed man himself.

About 1 a.m. Lilley began to talk loudly and wildly to Mrs Lilley. It was the rambling talk of a man with no control over his mind. Clarissa Lilley went to him, spoke softly and soothingly, trying to quieten him; but he raved on.

In desperation she turned to the sentry and asked him if he would go and call Sergeant-Major Cotton. There was a slight delay because Cotton had fallen and hurt his foot and could not come immediately. But Mrs Cotton came alone.

As she came into the sick man's room Lilley cried out:

'Come up on this side of the water, and not on that side.'

What rambling fragment of military memory this represented no one knows. It is simply something that impressed itself on the mind of the sentry, who recalled that Lilley 'also talked about dinner and supper, and other matters which showed that he was wandering in his mind'.

Lilley then leapt out of bed and immediately fell to the floor.

'Sentry, can you help, please?' called Mrs Lilley.

Ewing came into the bedroom and hauled the sergeant-major to his feet. Lilley struggled to free himself in his delirium and brought both himself and Ewing to the floor. Ewing put some wrestling hold on him and held him there until, in a little while, he calmed down and Ewing lifted him and got him into bed.

Mrs Lilley then poured out another half tumbler of brandy and brought it to Private Ewing with a teaspoon and asked him to give the brandy to her husband a spoonful at a time.

This was not an easy task for the sergeant-major was already slipping into a coma. Ewing stated: 'His teeth were closed, and I had some difficulty in giving it to him, but within five or ten minutes I managed to give him the greater part of the half tumbler of brandy. This seemed to make him easier, but he began to breathe very heavily from his chest: his stomach did not rise or fall, and Sergeant-Major Cotton, who came in just about this time, said he thought from the way he was breathing that he was very ill and they had better send for the doctor.'

There is a discrepancy between the statements of Private Ewing and Private Rutherford who was his relief at 2 a.m.

According to Ewing, after he had poured the greater part of half a tumbler of brandy into the sergeant-major with the spoon, Sergeant-Major Cotton told him to ride for the doctor. Ewing left but returned shortly afterwards unable to find a saddled horse to which Cotton had directed him. Meanwhile someone else had gone for the doctor.

Ewing said that Mrs Lilley asked him to stay with her in case her husband became violent again, and he remained until Dr Barnett arrived.

Rutherford speaks of arriving at the bungalow to relieve Ewing and seeing him 'standing near the head of the sergeant-major's bed with his left arm under the sergeant-major's neck, supporting his head.'

He recalls Ewing saying: 'You had better go and take my place; the sergeant-major's had a fit.'

Rutherford goes on: 'Ewing then went to a chest of drawers and brought out a tumbler containing a dram of what looked to me and smelt like brandy. The tumbler would hold about a third of a quart, and was nearly, but not quite, half full. There was a small teaspoon in the tumbler and Ewing poured the brandy into the sergeant-major's mouth by spoonfuls. He had some difficulty in doing this, as the sergeant-major's teeth were nearly shut close. His eyes were wide open and fixed on the ceiling, and he was breathing heavily from his chest, but there was no motion of the stomach.'

Was the glass of brandy that Mrs Lilley brought to Ewing the only brandy that he gave to Lilley, or did he, as is suggested by Rutherford, get a second glass himself and give that to Lilley also?

Dr Barnett arrived about 2.30 a.m. He felt Lilley's pulse and then shook him in an effort to rouse him. There was no reaction. The sergeant-major lay rigid, breathing with a loud gasping noise, eyes staring, face flushed, teeth locked.

'What's the matter? What's the matter?' the doctor shouted at him. There was no reply.

Dr Barnett turned to the small table in the bedroom and mixed something in a teacup which he brought to Lilley's side.

'Sergeant-Major, Sergeant-Major, open your mouth.'

There was no movement so Dr Barnett gripped Lilley's lower jaw and pulled it down a little. In this way he managed to pour the mixture into Lilley's mouth.

Rutherford, a no doubt fascinated observer, recalled:

'He appeared to swallow a little of it, but the greater part of it ran out of his mouth on each side.'

A few minutes later the apothecary, Mr Hudson, arrived from the camp hospital with his Indian assistants and, at the doctor's direction, lifted Lilley off the bed and laid him on the floor with a pillow under his head.

They bathed his head with cold water and applied a cooling spirit lotion to his head and chest: at the same time his feet were immersed in hot water and rubbed with mustard. This simultaneous application of hot and cold was intended to shock Lilley into consciousness, but it produced no reaction whatever.

Dr Barnett had a whispered conversation with the apothecary and then stooped over Lilley to make his last desperate bid to save his life. He applied a scalpel to the sergeant-major's left temporal artery to try to relieve the pressure in the man's head.

Rutherford, who was standing near Lilley's feet, saw:

'About half to three-quarters of a teaspoonful of blood flowed out, and Dr Barnett rose up and called for a bandage and bound up his head.'

But it was no use. Lilley did not move again, nor speak again, and the doctor recorded: 'He died comatose at 4 a.m.'

8

Verdict at Mhow

BEFORE passing to the concluding stage of the trial of Captain Smales the evidence of the adjutant, Lieutenant Fitzsimon, must be considered briefly.

Fitzsimon was called both by the prosecution and the defence. So far as his evidence for the prosecution was concerned, he was an unsatisfactory witness for Colonel Crawley. He did not fully support the colonel's suggestions that he had been present on the parades that were the subject of the trial.

The adjutant was vague in his recollections, and was clearly a reluctant witness for the prosecution. He was known to be on friendly terms with Captain Smales and continued to visit him at his quarters during the trial.

Fitzsimon said he did not see the colonel on parade on 1 May, 'although he may have been there'. The idea of an adjutant not knowing whether his commanding officer is present on parade or not may seem to military men to be bordering on the fantastic.

It would be tedious to go into the detailed evidence as to the colonel's presence, or otherwise, on parade. The fact remained that the adjutant's evidence, where it did not support the colonel, was obviously dangerous to him.

Colonel Crawley tried to dispose of the adjutant's doubtful recollection by telling the court in his closing speech:

'As every person acquainted with Lieutenant Fitzsimon knows that he is so blind that he cannot distinguish any person at five yards' distance so as to be sure of his identity, I leave the court to judge what value is his evidence as to my being on parade or not.'

This remark—without a single piece of evidence to support it—was, to say the least, a reckless attempt to discredit an inconvenient witness; and it was to have repercussions.

But the colonel was not yet finished with the adjutant. Dealing with the confinement of R.S.M. Lilley, Crawley said:

'Close arrest necessarily implies a sentry over a prisoner, but it does not necessitate his being placed over a prisoner's wife or family: and I can assure the court that no person could be more shocked than I was when I learned from the evidence of Sergeant-Major Lilley that his wife had been incommoded or annoyed by the precaution taken for *his* safe custody.

'It was Lieutenant and Adjutant Fitzsimon's fault, if any such thing occurred, for it was *his* duty, as adjutant, to have seen the post assigned to the sentry, and to have taken care that no such improper interference with the privacy of the sergeant-major's wife could have taken place.

'As it was, immediately I became acquainted with the statement of Sergeant-Major Lilley, I sent off orders to have the sentry removed to a post where he could perform his duty equally well without annoying or interfering with Mrs Lilley.

'With all the precautions, however, of having a sentry over him, Sergeant-Major Lilley did contrive to hold conversation and communication with a woman in the regiment, in contravention of the orders issued to the contrary.'

Colonel Crawley did not mention that Sir William Mansfield had informed him that there was no evidence on which the sergeant-majors could be convicted of conspiracy. He simply passed by their evidence as unworthy of notice: 'I put their evidence out of court altogether, as they have *all been guilty of a conspiracy* against me.'*

Without there having been the slightest examination of the conspiracy charge, this assertion was, of course, the exact opposite of the truth: they were guilty of nothing so far as the court was concerned, although whether their behaviour had been that of trustworthy senior N.C.O.s is another matter.

The colonel concluded his speech and the trial ended on 7 June 1862.

On this same day, possibly as Colonel Crawley was speaking, Mrs Lilley was painfully penning a last pathetic letter home:

'My dear sister and brother, This is indeed a painful moment

* Author's italics.

—a task I never expected to have to tell you. My beloved husband is no more. He died of apoplexy on the morning of the 25 May. It was so sudden; he was tolerably well the day before. Dear sister, in mercy go to our father and mother, I cannot write to them. The blow will be too much for them. I am staying with Sergeant-Major Cotton and Mrs Cotton. I was to have gone into hospital, but doctor says I shall not last long, so I don't think I shall be removed before anything happens. I cannot write any more, I cannot sit up. My best love. Your loving and affectionate sister, Clarissa Lilley. Mhow 7 June.'

The following day, a Sunday, Clarissa Lilley died of the disease that had been consuming her for so long. She was twenty-two years of age.

It was a busy weekend for Colonel Crawley. Somehow it came to his notice that the camp wine and spirit merchant had lost a good customer in R.S.M. Lilley.

He summoned the man, Ardaseer Framjee, to his house and there, in the presence of the acting adjutant, Lieutenant Davies, went through his books and drew up a detailed account of his recent transactions with Lilley.

Lilley's death had naturally been a source of great worry to the colonel, for the outcry in the press had been strident and sustained, and it was evident that things might not be allowed to rest as they were. Lieutenant General Mansfield had called, on 2 June, for full particulars of Lilley's death.

Dr Turnbull, in his report after carrying out a post-mortem examination of Lilley, said:

'The excessive heat at this season of the year, the constitutional predisposition of the deceased to congestion, the peculiar and painful circumstances of his position, the serious illness of his wife, causing depression of spirits, together with bilious and nervous derangement induced by the sedentary life attendant on close arrest in a man of the sergeant-major's active habits, probably acted as exciting causes to produce the complaint from which he died.'

So it may have been with some slight relief that on Sunday, 8 June, the colonel was able to write to Mansfield about his investigation of the wine merchant's dealings with Lilley.

He claimed that the wine merchant's account, which he enclosed with his letter, 'written in my presence by Ardaseer Framjee, Parsee merchant', showed that 'the unfortunate and misguided deceased had obtained and *must have drunk* within the short period elapsing between his arrest and his death from 26 April to 25 May, the inordinate quantity of 23 bottles of brandy, 12 pints of ale, two bottles of port wine, and one bottle of gin.

'It will also be apparent to His Excellency that, previous to his arrest the sergeant-major drank pretty freely, and that about the time he was engaged in concocting and siding in his conspiracy against me, viz between 6 and 26 April, he was liberally supplied with the maddening drink which caused his lapse from the path of duty and eventually his sudden death.

'It will not do for Surgeon Turnbull to ignore among the causes he assigns for that event, the influence of such an amount of fiery stimulant upon the frame of a man *violently predisposed*, according to his own account, to an attack of the disease which caused his death.

'It will be seen that Sergeant-Major Lilley drank the value of 57 rupees in various descriptions of liquor within the period of one month, or about *25 per cent more than his pay* for that time.'

The colonel also mentioned that in the course of conversation with Ardaseer Framjee the merchant had disclosed that Lilley was in the habit of visiting his shop daily and drinking two or three glasses of brandy for which the merchant did not charge him on account of his being such a good customer.

The next day, before despatching this letter, Colonel Crawley told Dr Turnbull and Dr Barnett of the amount of liquor sent to Lilley's bungalow.

He asked Dr Turnbull whether, in view of this, he wished to make any alteration in his report on Lilley's death.

The doctor replied that he did not, and he was quite certain that Lilley died of heat apoplexy, and he saw no reason to add anything since there was no proof that Lilley drank to excess or that drink was the immediate cause of death.

The colonel did not press the matter, although he may, rightly, have thought Turnbull was reluctant to do anything that might assist him in the trouble that was blowing up over Lilley's death.

But a few hours later Dr Turnbull had second thoughts. He wrote an addendum to his report, saying:

'In addition to the above, I wish to add that it has been brought to my notice that the deceased was in the habit of drinking a considerable quantity of brandy daily during the period of his arrest and, on enquiry, I find the above to be correct. It is my opinion that this, in connection with the other existing causes already stated, was calculated to increase the predisposition to apoplectic seizure from which he died. The universal reputation which the deceased enjoyed in the regiment for sobriety and steadiness, and the medical officer in his daily visits never having noticed any symptoms of intemperance, precluded all suspicion of his being addicted to the use of spirits.'

Dr Turnbull sent this note to Colonel Crawley, but it was returned to him by the adjutant with the information that 'Lieutenant-Colonel Crawley considers your additional or supplemental report to be unnecessary' and that the colonel's own report had been forwarded to Sir William Mansfield that morning.

The drink shown by the wine merchant's accounts was, of course, an enormous quantity and it put Lilley's death in an entirely different and, to the colonel, less embarrassing light.

If the sergeant-major had virtually drunk himself to death, his death could not be attributable entirely to the condition of his confinement, as the press accused.

The press attack on Crawley was fanned by Captain Smales, who wrote to the *Deccan Herald* giving an account of Colonel Crawley's ordering a twenty-four-hour watch to be maintained on Lilley. The abuse heaped upon the colonel in the newspapers went far beyond anything that could take place today without an action for libel being brought. The strictly proper silence, according to military regulation, that Crawley maintained in face of these attacks only encouraged their wider circulation.

The outcome of Captain Smales' trial was announced on Monday, 9 June.

He was found guilty on all charges and was sentenced to be

cashiered. This punishment is severe enough today with its total prohibition of re-employment in the government service, and the disgrace involved. But in Victorian times, with more rigid codes of conduct, it meant absolute social and professional ruin.

The sentence was confirmed a month later by Sir Hugh Rose, Commander-in-Chief, India.

Sir Hugh's comments on the case show that he totally adopted the prosecution evidence as the literal truth and paid, apparently, not the slightest attention to what was said by and in support of Captain Smales.

Sir Hugh's only criticism of Colonel Crawley was:

'It appears that on his assuming command of the 6th Dragoons he made a declaration to them, from which he did not depart, that he was very strict in all matters of duty, but that on all other occasions he wished to be on the best and most friendly terms with them.

'So far from having acted with undue severity, Lieutenant-Colonel Crawley appears to have treated his officers with great, indeed too much, forbearance on the many occasions when his authority was either questioned or resisted.

'The Commander-in-Chief, India, cannot approve the language which Lieutenant-Colonel Crawley addressed to some of the officers of the regiment on one or two occasions.

'Making every allowance for the trial to which his feelings were subjected as a commanding officer and a gentleman, His Excellency must think that it would have been better, in the interests of discipline and of his personal influence if, instead of making use of objectionable expressions with regard to certain officers, which produce irritation but not conviction, he had at once on the first declaration of opposition to his authority, vindicated it by the adoption of decided measures.'

Sir Hugh Rose was the living embodiment of harsh, unrelenting discipline. He had been the most distinguished general during the Indian Mutiny, and was an intimate friend of the Viceroy, Lord Canning. Any military matter that received his personal approval was virtually unassailable.

Sir Hugh was a man who found himself able to approve a death sentence on a private in the 5th European Regiment for insubordination, and disbanded the regiment. On another occasion he recommended the removal of two brigadiers for failing to visit hospitals during an outbreak of cholera. He was a man of iron where discipline and duty were concerned, whatever the rank of the offender. The zeal of Colonel Crawley would have commended itself to Sir Hugh.

Just by his own standards, he was the last man who would have gone out of his way to upset the findings of a court martial on an officer for insubordinate conduct.

The fate of Captain Smales appeared to have been settled.

It is just possible that it would have been, and that his trial would have disappeared into the military archives—a mere incident in the history of the British army in India, meriting no second glance from authority or public opinion.

But the death of R.S.M. Lilley made such an unremarkable end to the captain's tribulations impossible.

The death, with the sympathetic circumstances surrounding it, lifted the trial of Captain Smales from the humdrum pettiness of a garrison squabble to the heights of human drama and emotion as the details of the Lilleys' deaths became known to the public, first in India, then in England.

Before leaving the comments of Sir Hugh Rose it is worth noting his reference to Lilleys' death. So far as the record of the trial goes, it appears that no mention of this tragic event was made.

Sir Hugh, while considering the death of Lilley something 'extremely to be regretted', could not understand 'how Surgeon Turnbull, in stating with so much detail its causes . . . all of which details tended to inculpate Lieutenant-Colonel Crawley, should have been ignorant of the fact that the sergeant-major, although in a state that required medical attention, had purchased for his use within the short period elapsing between his arrest and his death—that is from 26 April to 25 May—the extraordinary quantity of twenty-three bottles of brandy, twelve pints of ale, two bottles of port wine, and a bottle of gin; quite enough, in combination with Indian summer heat, to compromise the life of a man in exercise and rude health.'

So at this stage of the story the unfortunate Lilley was not only dead before his time, but publicly branded as a drunkard who had been largely responsible for his own death, for Sir Hugh Rose's comments were widely published in the newspapers.

Naturally, it soon became known that Colonel Crawley had supplied the evidence on which Sir Hugh had based his remarks about the drink supplied to Lilley, and Colonel Crawley became the most hated man in the British army.

The *Times of India* carried a report from its Mhow correspondent on 30 May 1862, five days after Lilley's death:

'The sudden death of R.S.M. Lilley calls loudly for enquiry, and enquiry must be had, open and public. This man has been deliberately sacrificed, and there has been all but a second sacrifice in T.S.M. Wakefield; in fact, this man's life, from all I can learn, is not yet safe.

'What have these men done? is the general cry here. Law, civil and military, has been openly and in the most wanton manner violated. Sir Hugh Rose is hardly the man to look over this—three most respectable non-commissioned officers incarcerated without trial, with sentries over them night and day for upwards of a month. Is this the way our British soldiers are to be treated? Who ordered the punishment? By whose sanction was it carried out? The public must know this: we demand to know it and Sergeant-Major Lilley's friends in England will demand it . . . no Lynch law nowadays. If Lieutenant-Colonel Crawley is unable to command the 6th Inniskilling Dragoons as those whom he succeeded managed to do, in God's name relieve him at once. . . . Do the Articles of War mean what is written in them? Is a reign of terror to be the order of the day when men cannot command their regiment by legitimate means?'

Strong though this report from a correspondent was, the *Times of India* in a leading article the next day more or less openly accused Colonel Crawley of being responsible for Lilley's death.

The leader also gives an impression of the sergeant-major's funeral.

'Two-thirds of the men and most of the N.C.O.s of the regiment amongst whom he had lived for so many years, and by whom he was deservedly respected for his private and soldierly virtues, followed him to the grave. A great number of the N.C.O.s of Her Majesty's 72nd Highlanders and the Artillery were also present.

'It is scarcely necessary to add that Colonel Crawley was not present to witness the completion of his work. Considering the nature of the death of the deceased, we should like to know why no inquest was held, nor enquiry made into the particular circumstances under which it occurred. A verdict of manslaughter against the wretched man who has been guilty of the abominable tyranny would have brought the case within the jurisdiction of the Supreme Court.'

This was the kind of hard-hitting attack that went down very well with readers, who reacted strongly to what they knew of the facts.

A correspondent, who signed himself 'Dragoon', responded to the leader and, in so doing, gives a pathetic cameo of John Lilley's funeral.

'Your remarks in your paper of the 31 May about our poor old Sergeant-Major Lilley have been very thankfully read. When this infernal court martial began poor Lilley was a strong, healthy soldier, fit for anything and, I think, respected by everybody in the regiment. We are all glad to hear that some of our officers are going to put a monument over his grave.

'His funeral was a touching sight. His poor wife, who they say is in consumption, would go to his funeral. There she sat on the mound of earth covering two of her children, and the ground seemed ready to open to receive her next. I do not believe at this moment there is a man in the 6th Dragoons that doesn't look upon poor Lilley as an injured man.'

9

The adjutant's protest

CAPTAIN SMALES left Mhow to begin his journey home to England on 21 July 1862. He made no secret of his going, taking leave of his friends before he went but, understandably, he did not see fit to bid Colonel Crawley farewell.

What can his thoughts have been as he drove towards Bombay and a ship for England? The feud between him and Colonel Crawley had become almost an obsession with him, as it undoubtedly had with Colonel Crawley. Smales was determined to appeal, with legal advice, to the Queen if necessary. The last had not been heard of Captain Thomas Smales by any means; but it may be doubted whether he had much apprehension of further trouble before leaving India.

If this was so he was soon to be shaken out of his complacency. At Plasnee, on the road to Bombay, he was intercepted by an armed sowar—a native cavalryman—who handed him an official letter. This explained the sowar's presence and stated that, according to the military authorities at Mhow, Captain Smales had absconded with a deficiency of £1600 and he was to be arrested and brought back. It was the sowar's regretful duty to escort the sahib back to where he had come from.

Smales turned his back on Bombay and home and headed for Mhow and all that that place meant for him.

At Sindhwa, on the road back, there was another surprise for him. A native messenger rode up with another letter, this time written in Hindustani and intended for the sowar's information. This was to the effect that Captain Smales' arrest had been a mistake, that he was not to be molested, but he was to be asked to give up the first letter ordering, in English, his arrest.

Smales, being an old soldier, decided against handing over this piece of documentary evidence but, no doubt with relief, he turned again and retraced his way towards Bombay. This time he actually got aboard the steamer for England. But he was not to sail. Police came aboard with a magistrate's warrant and he was escorted ashore, charged again with absconding.

Captain Smales spent two months in custody while the law ground its way through its procedures. He repudiated all responsibility for regimental monies from the date of his arrest by Colonel Crawley prior to his court martial, because since that time he had been denied access to all his books and accounts.

A grand jury examined the charge against him and found no case for trial. There was, in fact, no deficiency and he was released.

Smales eventually reached England on 8 December 1862. He lodged at 126 Leadenhall Street, in the City of London, and reported his arrival to the War Office: it was a piece of military intelligence that may not have been received with excessive enthusiasm in Whitehall.

Meanwhile, in India, the reverberations from his trial could still be felt. Sir Hugh Rose's 'Remarks' were published on 3 September 1862 and Colonel Crawley's condemnation of his adjutant, Lieutenant Fitzsimon, over the position of the sentries, was echoed by Sir Hugh, who wrote:

'The evidence of Lieutenant and Adjutant Fitzsimon before the court was most evasive and unsatisfactory, and showed his entire unfitness for the adjutancy.

'To his carelessness and neglect of duty as adjutant must be attributed the annoyance caused by the posting of a sentry on the quarters of Sergeant-Major Lilley when that non-commissioned officer was directed by Major-General Farrell to be put in close arrest.'

Fitzsimon, who had served as adjutant for two years, was relieved of his position by Colonel Crawley on 23 May, before Lilley died and long before the end of the Mhow court martial; and it was a date that was to become important when Colonel Crawley himself was called to account before a military court.

But the publication of Sir Hugh Rose's remarks was the first intimation Fitzsimon had that Colonel Crawley's blaming of him for the annoyance of the Lilleys had been accepted and adopted by the Commander-in-Chief, India. It was, of course, an extremely damaging comment to be recorded against him unchallenged, and at an early stage in his army career.

Not much is known about Lieutenant Fitzsimon. He is rather a two-dimensional figure; not, it seems, a strong personality; not, it may be, and as Colonel Crawley claimed, a very efficient person in his military duties. But he may perhaps deserve some sympathy on being branded virtually a knave and a fool by the highest military authority in India, and an authority who had not deigned to question him on the matter.

Fitzsimon was on leave in Lucknow at the time Sir Hugh's remarks were published, and although they were printed in newspapers throughout India, Fitzsimon claimed not to have seen them and not to have been aware of the criticism until he heard about it on returning to Mhow.

However that may be, it was not until 3 November that he made a move to clear his name. He drew up a cautiously and respectfully worded letter to Sir Hugh Rose, denying the responsibility that Crawley had heaped upon him.

He claimed that in his actions concerning R.S.M. Lilley and his wife he had simply carried out the orders he received from his commanding officer; and he pointed out that these orders had been given in the presence of several witnesses who could be referred to.

He went on to say: 'I have, lastly, respectfully to observe that Lieutenant-Colonel Crawley, in his reply on the court martial, observes that I was so blind that I could not distinguish any person at five yards' distance so as to be sure of his identity. I must respectfully beg to assure His Excellency, Sir Hugh Rose, that I am not blind, and three medical officers who have examined my eyes testify that there is no abnormal appearance which might lead any person to suppose that I was blind.'

Finally, to counter a possible dangerous interpretation of his letter, he concluded:

'I most respectfully beg to state that I have taken the liberty to bring this matter before His Excellency through no feeling of disrespect or animus towards Lieutenant-Colonel Crawley, my commanding officer, but simply to remove the unfavourable impression of a supposed physical defect so ruinous to my future military prospects.'

Fitzsimon passed the letter to the acting adjutant, Lieutenant Davies, with a request for it to be forwarded through the normal channels to the Commander-in-Chief.

The first of these normal channels was, of course, his commanding officer, Colonel Crawley. It may be supposed that the colonel was somewhat disturbed by the letter. Was there to be no end to trouble from his subordinates?

He took no official notice of the letter for a fortnight so far as Fitzsimon was concerned; but he consulted with Major-General Farrell, the elderly divisional commander and author of the fatal order to put Lilley in close arrest.

Major-General Farrell decided to try to handle Fitzsimon on a personal and friendly basis rather than in an official way. He sent for the lieutenant and, as he put it later, 'I advised him, as a friend, not to send on his letter'.

The general told the lieutenant that he thought the letter would displease Sir Hugh and that wouldn't do at all, would it; but, of course, the lieutenant wasn't to think he was being *ordered* not to send the letter. He must distinctly understand that the general was simply giving his private advice on which Fitzsimon could act just as he pleased. If he wished it the letter would be forwarded at once.

Lieutenant Fitzsimon thanked the general and returned to the regiment.

He wrote a letter, and submitted it to Colonel Crawley, in which he requested leave to withdraw his first letter as Major-General Farrell considered that it was insubordinate.

This, naturally, would not do either. Colonel Crawley consulted with the general again and, on his return to the regiment, sent for Fitzsimon.

In his severest official manner, Colonel Crawley told Fitzsimon that he regarded his second letter as worse than the first one. He then read out part of a letter from Major-General Farrell's aide, intimating that the general thought the second letter ought to be withdrawn, and a third letter written in which there should be no mention of the reason why the lieutenant had decided to withdraw the original letter.

The lieutenant, possibly feeling that the odds were somewhat against him, wrote a formal non-committal letter requesting that his original letter be withdrawn.

Colonel Crawley must have thought that this source of worry and trouble had been effectively blocked.

Meanwhile trouble of a different kind, but due to the same causes, was building up for the colonel in England.

On 30 August, soon after the news of the result of the court martial reached England, the influential *United Service Gazette* took the matter up in a leading article.

'The sentence of the court martial in the long-protracted case of the paymaster of the Inniskilling Dragoons disposes of exactly one-half of that case in a satisfactory manner. There would be an end of all discipline and subordination in the army if paymasters were allowed to lecture their colonels upon regimental duty, and to answer charges against themselves by violent and irrelevant recrimination.'

The *Gazette* went on to point out that Smales would have been wiser had he accepted reproof on minor matters affecting his duty as paymaster, and worked strictly by the book so as to avoid his colonel's censure, and to have waited patiently for the proper time to take retaliatory action, if he thought such action advisable.

'Paymaster Smales has been cashiered, but what is to be done with Colonel Crawley?' asked the *Gazette*, rhetorically. 'Are we to have the words of Shakespeare once more verified, and to find that which was "rank blasphemy" in the subordinate is to pass as merely "a choleric word" in the commanding officer?

'Is no notice to be taken of the words, the proceedings, and the general deportment which were proved at the late trial? Is one of the finest regiments in Her Majesty's service to remain a hotbed of dissension and a military hell, in which an irresponsible Satan is to treat a whole community of officers and gentlemen as if they were so many *ames damnees*? . . .

'The erring paymaster has been visited with the utmost severity of the military law, but the sinning colonel has not, it appears, received even the mortification of a rebuke. . . .

'At present, few will deny the justice of Paymaster Smales' sentence, but if it be not followed by some retributive action in the case of his prosecutor, the curse of half-measures will oppress the whole decision and nobody, either in the service or out of it, will be satisfied with what has been done.'

This then was an unofficial military view of the affair. But civilian public opinion in England, although in agreement as to the need for some action against Colonel Crawley, was by no means satisfied that justice had been done to Paymaster Smales in the sentence meted out to him.

However, opinion outside the army had not yet had time to gain sufficient weight and momentum to force action upon the authorities.

Colonel Crawley saw in Sir Hugh Rose's 'Remarks' on the court martial a justification of his own conduct. He was instructed to read Sir Hugh's remarks to the regiment, and he did so on 18 September 1862. He chose the occasion to make a speech of his own which turned out to be more emotional than judicious.

The *Deccan Herald*, in reporting the speech—probably on a hearsay account of it—said that the colonel boasted to the regiment that the 'Remarks' were 'a victory' for him.

The speech inevitably came to the notice of Sir Hugh Rose, who called for a report on the matter from Crawley. Crawley, disputing the account in the *Deccan Herald*, said:

'I deny that I complained how badly I had been treated by my officers. I deny that I made any allusion whatever to the officers throughout the whole of my address, beyond what I read in the remarks of His Excellency, Sir Hugh Rose. No doubt some of these remarks were galling enough, but I deny that they were made more so by any comments of mine.'

The colonel enclosed with his report his recollections of his address to the regiment, which he said had been made without notes. It may be assumed that he did not goad his recollection to the extent of recalling his words in the least favourable form for transmission to the C.-in-C., so his 'transcript' from memory may be a comparatively sober and reasonable version of the original.

This then was what Colonel Crawley said to the regiment, according to his own recollection:

'Officers and soldiers of the Inniskilling Dragoons: It would not become me to add one word to the remarks of His Excellency, the Commander-in-Chief, India, which I have just read to you with reference to the court martial which has resulted as you have just heard; but I consider it due to myself and to the regiment in general to say a few words to you with respect to my own conduct in the trying circumstances in which I have been placed.

'It is now nearly seven months since the events which led to the proceedings took place—seven long and weary months have they been to me; of sorrow and anxiety, of mental disquietude and bodily labour, which I never can forget as long as my life lasts. During the whole of this miserable time I have been subjected to obloquy and infamous accusations, published against me in the newspapers of this country such as few men have ever had to submit to, and which I see by the newspapers received by the last mail, are being reproduced and repeated by the press at home.

'Scarcely a crime named in the decalogue but I have been accused of committing it, and my reputation as an officer and my character as a gentleman has been maliciously and recklessly assailed. During the whole time I have been content to sit still and to make no response to the horrible calumnies disseminated against me, though sorely tempted to do so by the provocation I received, and by the earnest advice and persuasion of my friends.

'I neither spoke myself, nor did I permit anyone to speak for me, satisfied that the day would come sooner or later when the whole truth would be known, and my character would be amply vindicated.

'That day has at length arrived, and in this document (here I held up above me the general order containing Sir Hugh Rose's remarks which I had just read) is contained the most ample and complete vindication of my conduct and character in every particular. Seldom, I think, has it fallen to the lot of any commanding officer to read at the head of his regiment a general order so complimentary to himself, or so eulogistic of his proceedings.

'His Excellency has said in these remarks that I have conducted myself with great, indeed too much forbearance on certain occasions when my authority was either questioned or resisted. That line of conduct I have now done with forever, and whenever I find the slightest spirit of insubordination or spark of indiscipline I will put my thumb on it and crush it out.

'The Commander-in-Chief has rebuked me by saying that he could not approve of language I used on one or two occasions. I bow with humility to His Excellency's rebuke, for I am one of those who consider the use of objectionable language, on any occasion whatever, a thing to be avoided if possible; but there are occasions in life when it is almost impossible to maintain that equable and unruffled temper which alone can prevent its use, and I venture to affirm that there are few commanding officers whose conduct, in this respect, would better bear the scrutiny which mine has undergone.'

The colonel then went on to make some fulsome remarks to the men, praising their bearing and morale.

This lengthy speech, even in its recollected form, is revealing of the man who made it: it ranges from self-pity to self-satisfaction, and from complacency to bombast and threats.

It was far from commending itself to Sir Hugh Rose, and his annoyance with Crawley is obvious in the reply which he instructed his Adjutant General to make to Sir William Mansfield, for onward transmission to the colonel.

'I am commanded by Sir Hugh Rose to request that Your Excellency will be so good as to inform Lieutenant-Colonel Crawley that he considers the address, such as he himself reports to have made to the regiment on this occasion, injudicious and entirely unnecessary. That it was unnecessary is admitted by the Lieutenant-Colonel himself in the beginning of the address.

'The Commander-in-Chief cannot refrain from observing that he the more regrets that Colonel Crawley should have made the address, for one part of it exhibits a return to the tone and language of which His Excellency expressed his disapproval in the remarks on the trial of the late Paymaster Smales which he Lieutenant-Colonel Crawley, had just read to the regiment. (Signed) E. Haythorne, Colonel, Adjutant General.'

Colonel Crawley must have been slightly chastened by this high-level disapproval of his conduct. He was still suffering from public obloquy over the death of R.S.M. Lilley, because it was soon made known that the enormous amount of liquor delivered to the Lilleys was not primarily for the sergeant-major's consumption at all, but to sustain his dying wife.

As Dr Barnett was to testify later in England:

'She was suffering from extreme exhaustion. The great irritability of her stomach and bowels did not admit of her taking solid food or nutritious broths. Four or five glasses of brandy were not too considerable a quantity for her to take.'

This fact was not known to Sir Hugh Rose when he wrote his 'Remarks', but it was known in December 1862 when the report on the court martial was being considered in Whitehall by His Royal Highness, the Duke of Cambridge, Commander-in-Chief of the Army.

The duke issued a public memorandum on the trial which reached India early in 1863. In it he wrote:

'This trial of Paymaster Smales has exposed a state of things in the Inniskilling Dragoons which His Royal Highness will endeavour to take an impartial view of. There is no doubt that the Inniskilling Dragoons under Colonel White and his successor, Colonel Shute—two distinguished officers in whom His Royal Highness has great confidence—before their embarkation for India, were all that could be desired as to *esprit de corps*, unanimity, and good feeling among the officers, and as to drill and discipline among the men.

'On their embarkation for India some changes took place among the officers, and the regiment had not been long in India when some unfavourable reports of the behaviour of one or two individuals when off duty, or at the mess, called down His Royal Highness's severe displeasure, the more so that it formed so strong a contrast to the previously acquired reputation of the corps.

'Still, with such exception, the regiment remained in the highest state of discipline, as elicited from all the confidential reports that have reached His Royal Highness from the Commander-in-Chief and inspecting general officers in Bombay, till Colonel Shute was succeeded by Lieutenant-Colonel Crawley from another corps.

'In permitting Lieutenant-Colonel Crawley to succeed Colonel Shute, His Royal Highness believed he had placed—

and he did, in fact, place—at the head of the Inniskillings an officer of experience in the lower ranks of the service, of considerable talent, knowledge and zeal; but unfortunately, as has been proved, an officer not gifted with the special talent which unites with the firmness of command the tact which inspires confidence and creates goodwill.

'From the first Lieutenant-Colonel Crawley appears to have taken an unfavourable view of some points in the regiment, and to have expressed himself in no measured terms as to the changes he contemplated, which His Royal Highness cannot but think was uncalled for and unnecessary, and which was sure to create an unfavourable feeling on the part of the regiment.

'The conduct of Lieutenant-Colonel Crawley subsequent to the court martial, if the address he made to his regiment—both officers and men—be correctly reported, was, to say the least of it, exceedingly reprehensible and injudicious. There are other points in Lieutenant-Colonel Crawley's conduct of which His Royal Highness cannot speak in too strong terms.

'His Royal Highness alludes to the confinement, under arrest, of certain non-commissioned officers during the trial, under a charge of conspiracy, which was never attempted to be proved against them, and for which there seems not to have been a shadow of foundation.

'His Royal Highness has also reason to believe that, had the Commander-in-Chief, India, been better acquainted with some of the facts of Sergeant-Major Lilley's case, he would have taken a different view of it from that which his remarks prove him to have done, and would not have attributed the death of that unfortunate non-commissioned officer to excess.

'Under these circumstances, nothing but the high opinion expressed of Lieutenant-Colonel Crawley by his general officers in immediate command has induced His Royal Highness to continue him at the head of the regiment, and he does so only upon trial, and under the hope that for the future he will be able to carry on discipline without outraging the feelings of the gentlemen under his command.'

There could hardly have been a stronger rebuke of a commanding officer, short of military legal action being taken against him, and that action, at this stage of the events, was not officially contemplated. Only public opinion would in due time bring that about.

Unknown to the public, the Duke of Cambridge wrote a private memorandum to Sir Hugh Rose and Sir William Mansfield, who were both implicated in the odium of the Mhow court martial.

The duke acquitted them both of everything except a desire to maintain discipline by supporting a commanding officer as far as possible.

'At the same time', he wrote, 'it is absolutely necessary that it should be made evident that those attaining high and responsible position, such as the command of a regiment of high repute, should understand that they are to exercise their functions with discretion, and refrain from seeking to exalt themselves by a depreciation of those entrusted to their command.

'These lessons, His Royal Highness hopes, have now been learned by Lieutenant-Colonel Crawley; and that he will, in future, by firmness united with temper and discretion, prove himself worthy to command a regiment which His Royal Highness knows, by personal experience, to have been equal to any in Her Majesty's service under former commanding officers.

'With respect to the long arrest of the non-commissioned officers, His Royal Highness sees no reason to alter his opinion of its impropriety, which is admitted by Sir William Mansfield, whilst he explains the causes.

'The case of R.S.M. Lilley will ever remain an unfortunate event. It is possible, perhaps probable, that he may have taken a portion of the liquor supplied for his wife, but there seems no proof that he did so to such an extent as to cause his death.

'His character for sobriety and correct conduct previous to his arrest seems to have been undoubted. In closing the correspondence on this painful subject the Field Marshal desires to express his hope that the conduct of all parties in the Inniskilling Dragoons for the future may be such as to deserve the approbation of the general officers under whom they may be called upon to serve; but should, unfortunately, what has passed not have been a sufficient warning to them His Royal Highness will not hesitate to visit with his severe displeasure those who forget their duty in the pursuit of their private animosities.'

10

A struggle for justice

In thinking that with his private memorandum he was 'closing the correspondence on this painful subject' the duke was very much mistaken. From December 1862 throughout most of the following year Whitehall departments—the Horse Guards, War Office, Judge Advocate General's office—were conducting a defensive paper war with the legal representatives of the Lilley family; with Captain Smales and his advisers; with the Indian military authorities, to say nothing of the continuous press publicity over the affair.

Captain Smales was a public martyr, disgraced, dismissed, denounced by the army but doggedly seeking justice in full public view.

Soon after his arrival in England he wrote at considerable length to the Duke of Cambridge, detailing his complaints at the treatment he had received from Colonel Crawley. He received a brief and noncommittal reply from Whitehall. '. . . His Royal Highness is compelled to remark that, even supposing those grievances to have had a real existence, he is quite unable to see how they can in any way invalidate the legality of your conviction by the court martial before which you were arraigned.'

This may have dismayed Captain Smales, but it did nothing to deter him. He was an inexhaustible and fluent letter writer and he tirelessly assailed the military offices of Whitehall with his demands for justice.

But by May 1863 there is a note of desperation in his writing. He complains to the Military Secretary:

'For several months past I have officially, in writing and in verbal communications addressed to yourself and the Adjutant General, complained of the course pursued by Lieutenant-

Colonel Crawley as prosecutor on my recent trial by General Court Martial.

'I have several times applied to have this and other objections brought under notice of the Judge Advocate General and I have indicated that I have been legally advised that the course pursued was illegal. Up to the present moment I have never received any reply whether this legal consideration of my case has taken place. . . .

'I have been frequently informed by yourself and the Adjutant General that I am not considered as guilty of falsehood and malice; that I was tried for and convicted of insubordination in writing the letter. . . . I am advised that, looking at the charge and its three counts in connection with the trial and evidence, that this view cannot be sustained.

'The insubordination described in the charge consisted in "having made false and malicious statements". The falsehood and malice was not proven, the gravamen of the charge fell to the ground. . . .

'I have brought evidence to prove that my witnesses were tampered with, threatened, and imprisoned without charge or trial: they were brought into court as prisoners in charge of a sentry without any charge recorded against them; clandestinely examined; threatened to be put in irons, and therefore necessarily gave their evidence under intimidation; that the prosecutor employed my own witnesses to procure evidence for his prosecution; that his own servant Private Walsh was employed in nocturnal visits to the barracks canvassing for evidence; that he issued an order preventing—and did prevent—me having access to my witnesses during my defence while he himself assembled the men of the regiment at his own house to examine them, and secure their testimony. . . .'

The War Office was not only troubled by the persistence of Captain Smales: there had been also a threat of civil proceedings against Colonel Crawley by R.S.M. Lilley's brother. No decision had yet been made concerning official action against the colonel, but this threat prompted an enquiry into the legal position.

The opinion of the Judge Advocate General, Thomas Headlam, was sought about whether it had been legal for the three

Lieutenant-Colonel Thomas Robert Crawley of the 6th Inniskilling Dragoons

Captain Thomas Smales, Paymaster of the 6th Inniskilling Dragoons, and architect of his own misfortune

General George Macdonald, Governor of Sierra Leone during the 1840's. The General, father-in-law of Captain Thomas Smales, always wore a specially-made high collar to hide an ugly wound he received as a young officer at Waterloo

Lord Sandhurst who, when he was Lieutenant-General Sir William Mansfield, gave the order which led to Lilley's death

BELOW *Sir Hugh Rose (right) with Lord Clyde whom he succeeded as Commander-in-Chief, India. Photograph taken during the Indian Mutiny*

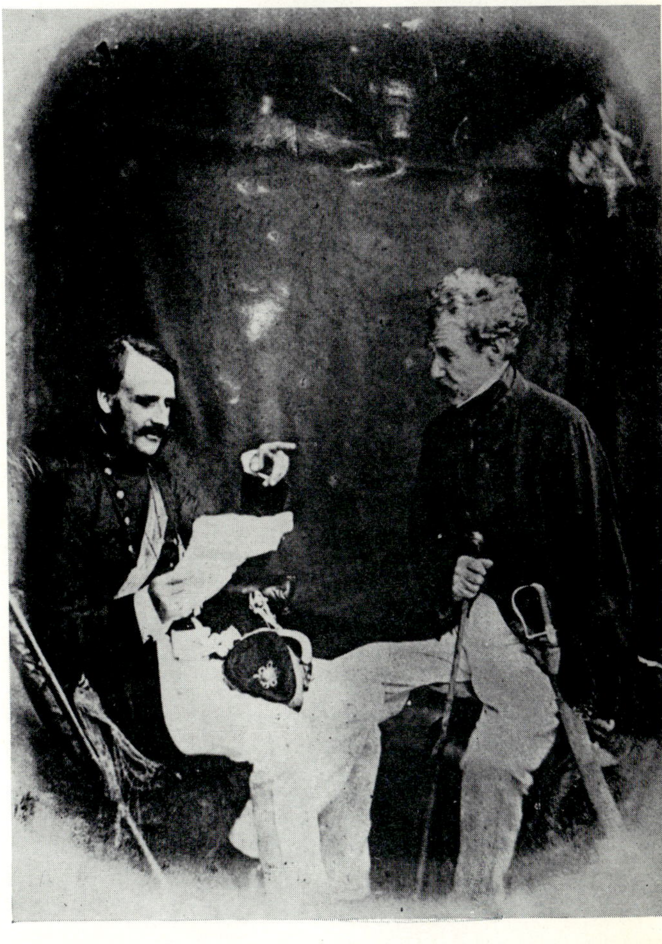

Colonel Sir Alfred Horsford, prosecutor at Crawley's court martial

LEFT *Duke of Cambridge, Commander-in-Chief of the British Army, as he was about the time of the Mhow court martial*

BELOW *An officer (right) gives evidence at the foot of the long table at which the court sits. Standing (left) by the small table is Colonel Horsford, the prosecutor. Lieutenant-Colonel Crawley is standing (right) with his legal advisers (seated) at the table on the opposite side of the court*

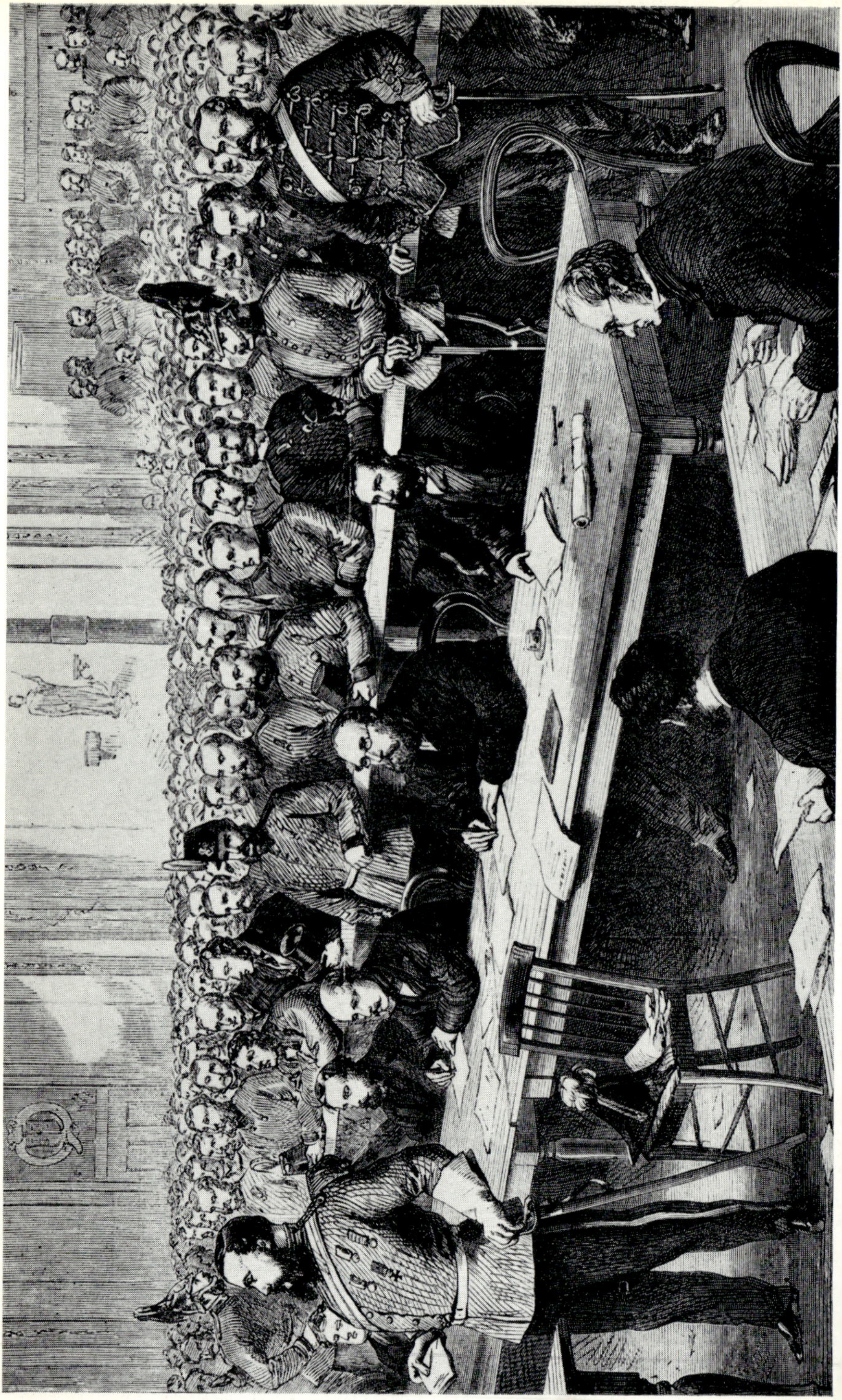

The inscription on the tomb of Regimental Sergeant-Major John Lilley and his wife

LEFT *The church of the British garrison at Mhow in 1862 adjoining the cemetery where the Lilleys were buried*

ABOVE *Quartermaster Charles Wooden,* V.C., *giving evidence during the court martial. Behind him is the press table*

Lilley's tomb in the old British cemetery at Mhow, photographed 1967 by Lieutenant-Colonel Na Salick, VR.C., *Indian Army*

sergeant-majors to have been kept in arrest without charge beyond the maximum of eight days laid down in the regulations.

The Judge Advocate, in a long and judicial reply, referred to the reasons advanced by Lieutenant-General Sir William Mansfield for keeping the sergeant-majors in custody.

It will be recalled that these were: so that they should be kept out of further temptation to conspire against their commanding officer; so that they should not be 'tampered with'; and so that their conspiracy should not appear to be condoned by their release before Captain Smales' trial was concluded: and all this without a charge ever having been brought against them.

The Judge Advocate commented: 'It is difficult to see how any, or all three of these grounds can be deemed sufficient to warrant the continuance of the arrest. Sir William Mansfield had already decided that there was up to that time no proof of conspiracy. And as that was the only ground on which the original arrest rested the three prisoners, in the opinion of Sir William Mansfield, were then under arrest on no charge that could legally be maintained. . . .'

Dealing with the three grounds put forward by Sir William Mansfield, the Judge Advocate was scathing: 'It need scarcely be said that military law does not empower a commanding officer to imprison a man to save him from being tempted to commit a crime.'

As to preventing Lilley's being tampered with, Mr Headlam found it 'difficult to understand precisely what is meant to be conveyed by these words. But if the meaning is that they were to be kept in close arrest in order to prevent Paymaster Smales communicating with them with a view to adducing them as witnesses for the defence on his trial, such a proceeding was, in my opinion, not only illegal, but was an act of arbitrary power having for its object an interference with the administration of justice. . . .'

On the third ground the Judge Advocate was equally forthright:

'The idea intended to be conveyed here seems to be this, that as a charge of conspiracy had been made against these three men which, up to that time, was not capable of being supported, they were not entitled to be released but might legally be detained in custody because a certain judicial enquiry was going on in the course of which more facts might possibly come out which might serve to throw some light on the conduct of these men, and might be made the foundation of that charge of conspiracy which, at that time, was admitted to be untenable.

'If this interpretation of this third reason be correct, I cannot see that it affords any justification for the continuance of the arrest of these three men.'

It was clear, in the opinion of the Judge Advocate, that Sir William Mansfield, as the senior officer concerned, had acted illegally in keeping Lilley and the others in arrest without any charge being brought: and on this question of legal responsibility Major-General Farrell and Lieutenant-Colonel Crawley were covered by Mansfield's order, little as he had known of the true circumstances of the arrest.

Captain Smales continued his struggle for justice throughout the first half of 1863, and was not officially cashiered until the notice appeared in the *London Gazette*, proclaiming his disgrace, on 30 May.

Earlier that month he was present at a royal levee at St James's Palace. It was not a social event to which he would normally have been invited, but he went in the company of Major-General W. F. Forster, the Military Secretary, who had dealt with the Duke of Cambridge's correspondence throughout the Mhow affair and had taken a special interest in Smales' case. The general personally arranged for Smales to be included in the list of invitations.

Smales wrote of him in his diary: 'Nothing could have been kinder than the general's behaviour towards me: he desired me to "tell the duke all you have told me. I know he wishes to serve you, and I am sure he will do you justice".'

Smales was the last of 150 officers to be presented to the duke, who, as Commander-in-Chief of the army, was the most powerful military man in the country. It was convenient for Smales to be last so that they could have a few words in private.

'Ah yes, Captain Smales.' The duke, a bulky figure with heavy moustaches and side whiskers, was naturally courteous to this insignificant, if not unknown, captain whose narrow-mindedness and stubbornness had brought ruin upon himself and grave trouble in high military places.

But today was a levee, and some unbending in official attitudes was perhaps not out of place.

'Your letter was, of course, a very improper one, Captain Smales.'

His Royal Highness went on to say that he had no desire to wound Captain Smales' feelings any further after all that had taken place, but he really 'ought not to have written such a letter'.

'I am sorry, your Royal Highness, that I did write it,' answered Smales, no doubt with truth, 'but I was driven to it, as it were in desperation, by Lieutenant-Colonel Crawley's conduct. He shook his fist at me and behaved in a manner that no gentleman could possibly submit to.'

Encouraged certainly, and flattered perhaps, by being received by the duke, Smales went on to deny that his letter was false. 'But as I now stand I am convicted of being a liar and a slanderer, neither of which was in the remotest degree proved.'

The duke resumed his official mantle and rumbled in reply:

'No, Captain Smales, that is not it: your letter is not considered false—it was insubordinate.'

Smales does not record what, if anything, he replied and, in the circumstances, it may be assumed that the conversation was not prolonged.

Smales' formal written battle with Whitehall and, ultimately, with the Duke of Cambridge himself, continued. The announcement of his cashiering was merely an incident, an inevitable result of his court martial since no sufficient grounds had yet been produced to the Commander-in-Chief for staying it. It is doubtful whether the duke could have interfered with the formal notice in the *London Gazette*, whatever else might have come to his attention, for the India command differed from every other overseas military station in that, once a sentence had been confirmed by the Commander-in-Chief, India, it was absolute; there was no machinery within the army for overriding his decision.

Smales, of course, was seeking a free pardon from the Queen and on 9 June the Judge Advocate brought that possibility a stage nearer when he wrote to the War Office, pointing out that as the arrest of the three sergeant-majors was illegal and Smales was not allowed to communicate with them as defence witnesses—while Colonel Crawley had invited the court to disregard their evidence on the ground that they were guilty of conspiracy—'It appears to me difficult to say that the proceedings were not thereby vitiated altogether. . . . I have therefore the honour to submit, for the consideration of His Royal Highness, whether he should not be pleased to recommend Her Majesty to grant Mr Smales a free pardon.'

The Duke of Cambridge was not a man to accept legal recommendations simply because they were offered by an eminent legal authority, and he raised the point whether it had been actually proved that Smales had been *denied* access to the sergeant-majors as witnesses for his defence.

Enquiries were made by the War Office of Lieutenant Fitzsimon, the former adjutant, whether Smales had ever *requested* permission to communicate with the three imprisoned men. It turned out that Smales had not asked formally to be put in touch with them.

It may be thought, on what is now known, that the possibility of such a request being granted to him during the Mhow court martial would never have occurred to Smales. There is scarcely any doubt that it would have been refused—since to prevent such communication was a main purpose of the arrests.

The Judge Advocate was evidently of the same opinion; and perhaps he may have been slightly nettled that his considered opinion was being questioned to this extent by the duke.

He wrote, as his final word on the subject—although he did not, of course, put it quite like that—'I think the manner in which the witnesses for the defence were treated by the prosecutor was contrary to the principles of justice and made the trial substantially an unfair one . . . it is impossible to say whether the manner in which these witnesses were treated did, in this particular case, affect either the verdict or the sentence; but I am certainly of opinion that such a mode of conducting a prosecution is wrong, and that the omission of Mr Smales to make a formal application to see his witnesses is not a matter of sufficient consequence to affect the conclusion.'

This, of course, answered the duke's query but he was, apparently, still not too happy about Captain Smales' being granted a free pardon. Perhaps it seemed too much as if Smales would be getting away with everything if a pardon were to restore the *status quo* to that existing prior to the Mhow court martial.

The duke therefore asked the Judge Advocate what Smales' position would be if he *were* pardoned; would he 'resume his position of paymaster of the 6th Dragoons, or be a paymaster without being attached to any corps, or placed on the half-pay list?'

This was the first step by which Smales was to be pardoned —but at the same time continue to be punished. The Judge Advocate appears to have sensed what was in the duke's mind, for he outlined the hypothetical position of Captain Smales, were he pardoned, in this way:

'If a pardon is granted to Mr Smales and nothing whatever is done with respect to his reinstatement, he will not be paymaster of the 6th Dragoons, nor be entitled to full pay in that capacity, or in the capacity of paymaster of any other regiment; neither will he be entitled to half-pay unless placed on the half-pay list.'

The Judge Advocate thought it would not be advisable for Smales to return to the 6th Dragoons as paymaster, and while he hesitated to give his opinion on what was a purely military matter, he thought that if Captain Smales' pardon were to incorporate a condition that he should not be reappointed to the 6th Dragoons 'such a declaration would prevent any claim or demand being made on his behalf for his reappointment'.

This opinion was given on 4 July 1863 and it appeared to reassure the duke, for by 21 July the procedure for a Queen's pardon had been completed and Smales was informed of this improved turn in his fortunes.

He lost no time: within a week he applied to be paid in the

rank to which he assumed he had been restored. He explained that he had a very large family dependent upon him, that he had had to pay his own fare to England, and that he had not been paid since 30 January 1862.

He received a very cool reply from the War Office, dated 26 August 1863, which disclosed the curious nature of the pardon which had been granted to him.

'In reply to your letter of the 30th ultimo, in which you request with reference to Her Majesty's pardon which has recently been granted to you, that you may receive your pay as paymaster and that your name may be noted for immediate active employment, I am directed to acquaint you that the Secretary of State for War has been advised that the pardon which Her Majesty has been pleased to grant you has left you in the position of a civilian. I am therefore to inform you that you are not entitled to receive any pay and, further, that it is not the intention of Earl de Grey and Ripon* to submit your name to the Queen for an appointment as paymaster.'

Smales immediately sent a copy of this astonishing letter to the press and it was printed in *The Times* on 31 August 1863. It naturally aroused a good deal of interest because other aspects of Captain Smales' court martial were very much under public notice now, the matter having been taken up in parliament.

The Times came to Captain Smales' defence in a leading article.

' "Consider yourself horse-whipped" is a well-known formula', the leader began, 'and anyone to whom it is addressed knows perfectly well what it means. It is a compendious form of challenge which must either be accepted or treated with contempt. But the War Office seems to have invented a new formula which seems to amount to this: "Consider yourself pardoned." '

Recalling the circumstances of Smales' court martial, his formal pardoning and the recently published letter from the War Office to Smales, the writer went on: 'In other words, Mr Smales, having been illegally cashiered, is to consider himself pardoned but is to remain in precisely the same condition and subject to precisely the same penalties as if he had

* Secretary of State for War.

been legally cashiered and had received no pardon. It appears, therefore, that this unfortunate gentleman has been pardoned and has not been pardoned, has been cashiered and has not been cashiered . . . it cannot have escaped the recollection of many that Colonel Crawley himself, after being severely rebuked by the Commander-in-Chief, was still allowed to retain his command in order that he might retrieve his character. Such an indulgence would have been more just had it been extended to Mr Smales.'

Gradually, in face of public opinion and the impossibility of making a free pardon anything less than it had always been held to be, officialdom relented and in November 1863 the law officers of the Crown made their final adjudication on Captain Smales. They advised the Secretary of State for War: 'We think it would be expedient and proper that Her Majesty should be advised to place Mr Smales on half-pay at the rate of 6*s* per diem, being the rate to which he would be entitled if he had continued to serve as paymaster down to the present time, and had now been incapacitated from further service.

'The circumstances are very exceptional and such as to warrant in our opinion such an exercise of Her Majesty's power. And we see no further way in which the fair requirements of justice can be reconciled with the interests of the public service.'

It had been a long struggle, and if he had not struggled personally it may be doubted whether Captain Smales would ever have been anything more than a disgraced, cashiered officer after the court martial at Mhow. But, due mostly to his own efforts, he had, by the end of 1863, come a long way back along the road to re-establishment of his position.

II

The Mhow scandal exposed

INTERESTING as Captain Smales' position was to the general public, by far the greater interest centred upon the villain of the drama, Lieutenant-Colonel Crawley. Although there had been a great deal of activity behind the scenes in Whitehall, it was not until 5 June 1863 that the matter was raised in parliament and the government were obliged to take formal notice of the state of affairs in the 6th Inniskilling Dragoons.

Mr Dudley Fortescue, M.P. for Andover, gave the first detailed narrative of the Mhow court martial, and the facts he related sent a sensation of horror and anger rippling through the country. The details of the affair had at last burst beyond the esoteric confines of military journals.

Mr Fortescue outlined the events leading up to the arrest of the sergeant-majors, and then asked rhetorically:

'What does the 99th Article of War say with respect to confinement? It says: "When any soldier or officer commits an offence deserving punishment, he shall be ordered into arrest or confinement until released by lawful authority, and no officer or soldier shall continue in such arrest or confinement more than eight days, or until such time as a court martial can conveniently be held."

'And the 79th Article says: "Whosoever shall unnecessarily detain any prisoner in confinement without bringing him to trial, shall, if an officer, be liable to be cashiered or to suffer such other punishment as, by the judgment of a general court martial, may be awarded." '

The loud cries of 'Hear, hear' from the crowded Commons benches showed how a substantial number of members felt about the activities of Colonel Crawley. But if their emotions were aroused already, there was a stronger stimulus to come

Mr Fortescue continued: 'But these men were kept in confinement not for eight days, but for several weeks; one was liberated only by death, and when the order for release came for the other two, it found one of them a raving lunatic, and he was conveyed to the hospital suffering from brain fever.

'After four weeks' imprisonment Sergeant-Major Lilley was taken ill, and he died within a few hours. No inquest or committee of enquiry, which would be there the equivalent of an inquest, was held, but a post-mortem examination was made by the regimental surgeon who certified that the cause of death was apoplexy, brought on by his sedentary life and the peculiar circumstances in which he was placed.

'The place where Sergeant-Major Lilley was confined was a single room in a bomb-proof building, formerly used as cavalry stables and which have since been pulled down as unfit for the occupation of troops. It was impossible that the roof of this building could get cool, the amount of heat collected in the day could not be carried off by night.

'In a room, then, more like an oven than a human habitation, was Sergeant-Major Lilley imprisoned, and this room was shared by his wife who was confined to her bed by a diarrhoea attending the last stage of consumption. She only survived her husband two or three weeks.

'A sentinel was placed over the sergeant-major with injunctions to keep him in sight, and not to allow him to receive any communications from without. In consequence of a sergeant's wife having attempted to communicate with the sick woman, Colonel Crawley, incredible as it might appear, ordered the sentry to be stationed inside the room, and there, in the presence of strange men, renewed from day to day, and posted three feet from her bed, all the functions of nature had to be performed by this dying woman.'

It requires little imagination to conceive the effect a narrative of this kind would have on the public. All the emotion-rousing details were there: the unsuccessful attempt to prove that Lilley had died of drink, the fact that the sergeant-major's wife had been kept alive only by large doses of wine and spirits.

'For redress and reparation it is unhappily too late,' Mr Fortescue went on. 'Lilley is dead, his wife is dead, his children are dead. But if it is too late for reparation it is not too late for punishment.'

Loud cheers, such as are indulged in comparatively rarely, echoed round the Commons chamber. They were renewed as Mr Fortescue added: 'Such punishment as I trust this House will force upon the authorities. The death of Lilley excited a very painful feeling in India, the matter was taken up by the press, and it became clear that it could not be confined to that country.

'It was at last brought under the notice of the Commander-in-Chief who, in his memorandum, while censuring Colonel Crawley, has with the most incomprehensible leniency, left him in a position for which he has shown himself so manifestly unfit.'

'Hear, hear,' said several members, warmly.

'Let the House mark the varying measure of justice dealt out according to the rank of the offender. Paymaster Smales, for writing a letter which was considered insubordinate, was brought to a court martial, tried and cashiered; while the commanding officer, acting with the greatest injustice and oppression, was visited with no severer punishment than a simple reprimand.

'But I cannot believe that in the face of such facts as have been brought forward, this strange leniency will be persisted in. I hope Colonel Crawley will not be left the power, as he has shown he has the will, to inflict tyranny and persecution on those beneath him.

'So persuaded are the sergeant's relatives that his blood lies at Colonel Crawley's door that I have authority for saying they are determined to indict him for manslaughter so soon as he appears in this country, unless the government take the matter up earnestly.'

This speech was nothing less than an inflammatory indictment of Crawley, and it undoubtedly played its part in the War Office's ultimate decision to bring Crawley to trial, for such charges could not be dealt with by parliamentary answers.

The Marquess of Hartington, Under Secretary for War in Palmerston's Liberal government, gave a factually correct and unemotional outline of the arrest of the sergeant-majors and how it had come about. He pointed out that both Colonel Crawley and Major-General Farrell were technically covered by the order of Lieutenant-General Sir William Mansfield.

In an attempt to explain and justify the apparent lack of action against all these officers the Marquess said:

'But the conduct of these officers and the illegality of the course they pursued is a subject which it will be perfectly in the power of the Commander-in-Chief, in conjunction with the Secretary of State, to point out to them, and bring under the notice of the army in such terms of reprimand and reprehension as might seem to be advisable.

'But what I wish to point out is that it is incumbent on His Royal Highness to act with the greatest care and caution when he is dealing with so distinguished an officer as Sir William Mansfield.'

There were 'hear, hears' denoting that Sir William had his supporters in the Commons, and proving the point made by the Marquess.

'If I am right in the view I have tried to place before the House, it will be evident to all that Sir William Mansfield acted under a misapprehension and that he is in no way mixed up with the miserable squabbles and petty jealousies which have distracted the 6th Dragoons. It must be evident that though wrong, Sir William Mansfield acted for what he supposed to be the best interests of the discipline of the army.

'Under these circumstances it is the duty of His Royal Highness to deal not only with care and caution, but also with the greatest moderation and leniency.'

There were ironical cheers from some members when the Marquess went on to announce that in view of the illegality of the confinement of the sergeant-majors, and the poor circumstances of Lilley's aged parents, who had been dependent upon him, the government had decided to make them a grant 'as would be about equal in amount to the pension to which the deceased would have been entitled had he received his discharge at the time of his death'.

On 8 June a Mr C. Pembruge Langston, no doubt having read the parliamentary report in the newspapers, wrote to the Duke of Cambridge from 384 High Street, Cheltenham, putting in a few words the feelings of many people in the country towards Colonel Crawley.

'Will you do me the honour (being too poor to obtain legal assistance) whether we, as friends of poor Sergeant-Major Lilley, can have Colonel Crawley arrested on his arrival in England on a charge of manslaughter. I cannot allow myself to express my feelings to you on the conduct of that brutal fellow, lest I should overstep the bounds of courtesy due to your Royal Highness.'

Perhaps awe at the rank of his correspondent caused Mr Langston to miss out a word or two, but the meaning is clear enough in this literal transcript of his letter.

The duke replied noncommittally that he 'could give no opinion on the matter as it is a question for civil law to decide'.

The matter came up again in the Commons on 12 June when, in spite of a plea by Lord Palmerston that it was better not to discuss the case in view of the decision to court martial Colonel Crawley, Mr W. Coningham, the member for Brighton, refused to remain silent.

'Is it not monstrous,' he said, 'that Paymaster Smales of the 6th Dragoons, for writing what was characterised as an insubordinate letter—the insubordination of which I must confess is, to me, by no means so patent as has been stated—should have been sent before a court martial in the manner in which he was, without any previous investigation, and the witnesses actually impounded who were in readiness to support his case? The whole proceeding was perfectly disgraceful.'

Mr Coningham stressed that two general officers were 'deeply implicated' in the matter.

This brought General Peel, the member for Huntingdon, to his feet protesting that 'it is not open to Mr Coningham to discuss the case of the court martial held on Paymaster Smales with reference to which he has given no notice, and of the proceedings of which the House has no record'.

The Speaker ruled that Mr Coningham was in order, and the member for Brighton returned to the attack, using General Peel's intervention as additional ammunition.

'The interruption of General Peel is entirely in accordance with the whole conduct of the military authorities in the cause to which I am drawing attention. They are all for suppression; but so long as I have the honour of a seat in this House I will not allow so monstrous an outrage to be perpetrated without protesting against it.

'In the name of the officers, non-commissioned officers and private soldiers of the British army I demand that justice shall be done, even though the persons to whom blame attaches in the transaction are general officers, and including among the number His Royal Highness, the Commander-in-Chief of the Army.'

There were shocked cries from various parts of the chamber as Mr Coningham brought the Duke of Cambridge into the area of his criticism. But he swept on, undeterred:

'It has been said that the House of Commons is a house of colonels and one would think from the groans of those who sit opposite that their sympathies are enlisted on the side of men who have deliberately and in cold blood, acted in the manner to which I am particularly to advert.'

Mr Coningham then went into some of the details of the affair. Perhaps his shade might agree, on a century's reflection, that his speech was intemperate, to put it mildly, but it exemplified the general feeling among the public based on the information about Mhow then available.

On 15 June, in the House of Lords, the matter was raised in the decorous, half-apologetic way that is customary in that House. The Earl of Shaftesbury gave notice of his intention to put down a question about Lieutenant-Colonel Crawley and Regimental Sergeant-Major Lilley.

He said he had no official knowledge of the matter, but thought 'whether right or wrong, so frightful a picture as that presented in the case I have alluded to has never yet been brought under the notice of the British public: and I must add that as far as I can judge, what has taken place hitherto is most unsatisfactory, and such, I believe, is also the judgment of the public. . . . I do not recollect in my experience any matter which has more profoundly moved the public feelings of the country.'

The Duke of Cambridge, making his first public statement in the affair since his memorandum on the Smales trial, said, in reply, that although the army in India was in a unique position and the Commander-in-Chief there had complete authority over court martial sentences, when the proceedings of the Mhow court martial were sent home as a matter of routine 'they struck me as being so remarkable that I thought I ought to review them carefully. I feel sure that Sir Hugh Rose and Sir William Mansfield had every desire to do their duty, but that they committed a very serious error of judgment.'

Excusing the delay in the matter, the duke pointed out that it took nearly three months to get an answer to any question that might arise in London out of documents sent from India. Whatever had been done had been done with a view 'not to screen any person, but with the strictest and most earnest desire to do justice to all . . . as to any pressure being brought upon me I, of course, spurn the idea'.

The inference was current among sympathisers with R.S.M. Lilley and his family that efforts were being made to hush up the affair and save Colonel Crawley from an enquiry into his conduct; the same implication had been made by Mr Coningham in the Commons.

The duke added: 'It does so happen that I have never discussed the matter with any single individual except in an official manner, and then only with those parties on whose judgment I was enabled to rely in coming to a sound, just and safe conclusion.'

It was a soothing and no doubt honest statement, designed to allay fears that there would not be a full enquiry in due course.

A fortnight later orders were sent out from the War Office to Sir Hugh Rose instructing him to send Colonel Crawley to England to face a court martial at Aldershot.

The military journals were particularly critical of Crawley.

The *Army and Navy Gazette*, which had remained silent for months about the reports it had been receiving from Mhow, finally spoke out on August 9 1862.

It called the treatment of Lilley, Wakefield and Duval 'The saddest and most horrible and most flagrant proceeding of all . . . Lilley . . . had a sick wife and two children with him. His wife could hardly communicate with the doctor on account of the proximity of the sentry placed over this prisoner, against whom no charge was preferred. After a month of this Lilley died, the cause being confinement and distress of mind . . . his wife and two children, we believe, have since died. Another of those imprisoned witnesses was taken raving mad to the hospital. All this is very horrible and very disgraceful.'

Here may be seen the kind of half-truth and garbled account of the happenings in India that were current in England, with inevitable prejudicial results on public opinion.

A week later, unaware that orders were already on their way to India to bring Colonel Crawley home for trial, the *Gazette* returned to the subject.

'It is beyond conception that Colonel Crawley's conduct should be passed over in silence, when he has been accused of outrages on discipline and on good feeling, with violations of truth, with setting a bad example in morals and language to his officers, and with acts of arbitrary and cruel severity towards non-commissioned officers whom he imprisoned lest they might give evidence against him. India is ringing with these charges. The clubs are full of them. It is only an act of justice to Colonel Crawley to give him an opportunity of refuting these accusations, and to brand with disgust the infamous slanderers who have combined to blast his good name; but it is a duty to the Service and to the country to see that he shall not be permitted to remain in his present position and to ruin a noble regiment, if a tithe of the charges against him be proved.'

Lieutenant-Colonel Crawley has been shown to have been a man of harsh and peremptory manner when about his duties; wanting in tact and judgment when dealing with his officers. The manner of his leaving Mhow at the end of August 1863 comes, therefore, as something of a surprise.

It was 9 a.m., 24 August, and Crawley had not yet breakfasted before taking the road to Bombay on his way to England. A Colonel Christie, of the 9th Native Infantry regiment, presented himself at the colonel's bungalow and told him that the men of the Inniskillings had turned out and were already waiting on the road near the church at Mhow.

'They have asked me if I would come and ask you to leave the station by way of that road,' he said.

Colonel Crawley had his breakfast and no doubt pondered on this unexpected message. There were still some matters to be attended to that morning, and it was 10.45 a.m. before the colonel, accompanied by Major Champion of the Mhow headquarters staff, was driven away from his bungalow.

It had been raining hard and as their carriage approached the church, where the Lilley family lay, Colonel Crawley became aware of men running from their quarters across the glistening wet ground to intercept him.

They gathered by the roadside—practically the entire regiment, and as the colonel's carriage drew near they gave several hearty cheers. The driver reigned in the horses, and Crawley looked out—for the moment his face set in its usual austere parade-ground lines.

It may be assumed that his mood had been sombre as he left his home, his mind preoccupied with the trying weeks to come —for he could have had no illusion that his entire future was not at stake. Was there to be an ignominious end to a lifetime of military service?

Then he realised what the men were shouting: 'God bless you, Colonel', 'Good old Crawley', 'We hope you'll soon be back', 'Good luck, sir'.

Colonel Crawley blinked slowly, and swallowed an emotion that came seldom to him. It was embarrassing, this kind of thing, and damned undisciplined—and nothing so wonderful had ever moved him so before.

He held up a hand and the men became silent. 'Thank you all,' he said, 'I can only trust that you will behave under my successor in the same soldier-like way that you have under me. Thank you and goodbye.'

The driver rustled the reins and the carriage moved on. Some twenty yards beyond the last man by the roadside the carriage moved between the wives and children of the regiment. Handkerchiefs fluttered, there were tears and more cries of 'Good luck'.

The journey home had had an auspicious beginning.

12

The charges are prepared

Two charges were drawn up against Lieutenant-Colonel Crawley by the Judge Advocate General, for approval of the Commander-in-Chief of the Army.

The first charge was originally drafted in this way: '... for conduct unbecoming an officer, and to the prejudice of good order and military discipline, in having at Mhow during the month of May 1862, *after having received an order from Lieutenant-General Sir William Mansfield, K.C.B., Commander-in-Chief of the forces in the Bombay presidency, to place R.S.M. Lilley under close arrest caused the said order* to be carried into effect with unnecessary and undue severity, whereby the said R.S.M. Lilley and his wife were subjected to great and grievous hardship and sufferings'.

This form of words did not find favour at the War Office for the obvious reason that it clearly stated that R.S.M. Lilley had been in close arrest by the order of Sir William Mansfield. It was much more satisfactory from the point of view of the military hierarchy that Sir William's specific connection with the affair should remain as unpublicised as possible; that the spotlight of notoriety should be focused sharply on Colonel Crawley alone.

As Mr Thomas Headlam, the Judge Advocate General, recorded, the charge was amended 'to meet the wishes of others'. The words in italics were taken out of the original charge and an insertion was made so that it read: '... in having at Mhow during the month of May 1862 when R.S.M. Lilley was confined in close arrest, caused the order under which he was so confined to be carried into effect etc., etc.'.

The second charge accused Colonel Crawley, during the court martial of Captain Smales, of having blamed the adjutant, Lieutenant Fitzsimon, for posting sentries in a way that intruded on Mrs Lilley's privacy 'whereas, in truth, and in fact, the said Lieutenant-Colonel Crawley then well knew that the said Lieutenant and Adjutant had acted in the said matter by the express order and direction of him, the said Lieutenant-Colonel Crawley'.

These charges were not to Colonel Crawley's liking at all. If he was going to be tried he wanted the whole affair to be gone into, for he was just as sure of the righteousness and rectitude of his own actions throughout as his enemies were of his vindictiveness, brutality and arrogance.

The colonel wrote to the Adjutant General from 5 Suffolk Street, off Pall Mall, on 14 October 1863:

'I have hitherto—in deference to the well-recognised rule of both the naval and military services which, on matters of duty, enjoins that no officer shall enter into a controversy with the public press—persistently abstained from in any manner noticing the attacks to which I have been subjected. Consequently, I have heretofore been unable to offer any explanation of my conduct, or to vindicate my character in any way whatever.

'Under these circumstances the perusal of the charges on which I am arraigned has produced in me a feeling of cruel disappointment, inasmuch as I am satisfied that the present charges will not enable me to give that account of my conduct which the justice of the case so imperatively demands.'

The Lilley family also thought the charges were too narrow, but for different reasons. Their solicitors wrote to the Duke of Cambridge requesting that the colonel be charged also with disobeying the Articles of War by imprisoning Lilley for so long without bringing him to trial.

They demanded that a more emotional charge be added accusing Crawley of 'highly disgraceful conduct' in denying Mrs Lilley a nurse or woman to attend her in her illness, compelling her husband to look after her and thus causing his death.

The duke rejected these requests in definite terms.

As the date of the trial drew nearer the controversy continued in the newspapers. The sergeant-major's brother, Mr Samuel Lilley, of Llandudno, wrote to *The Times* on 21 October at considerable length, defending R.S.M. Lilley against charges of drunkenness that had been openly made.

'. . . Last week remarks appeared in one of the leading London journals, as also a reproduction from an Indian paper in one of the military journals, imputing my brother's death to intemperance.

'It appears to me to be of little importance to the real points at issue as to *how* my brother died, or whether he died at all. The real question is, whether his commanding officer had a right to act towards him in direct disobedience of the Articles of War.

'That he died under such treatment was but an aggravation of the case: but Sir, these false and wicked statements naturally cause his family much distress, and this will, I hope, plead with you as a justifiable excuse for my begging of you to publish in *The Times* the enclosed extract of a letter written by Dr Turnbull, surgeon of the 6th Inniskilling Dragoons, referring to my brother's death.

'This extract has been many months in my hands and a copy of it was forwarded to the Horse Guards and its existence is, therefore, perfectly well known.

' "With regard to poor Sergeant-Major Lilley's case, Colonel Crawley has done all he could to prove he was a drunkard, and was furious with me because I would not side with his views. Dr Barnett and I frequently saw him during the period of his arrest, and never saw him the least the worse for drink. I believe the poor fellow died of a broken heart from the ill usage he received from the Mhow and regimental authorities."

'This is a literal copy. I repeat, the Horse Guards are in possession of it and I ask, as a favour to myself and family, the publication of this defence of my brother's character which has been wantonly assailed.'

It is not clear how this letter from Dr Turnbull, or a copy of it, reached Mr Samuel Lilley.

The letter was written at Mhow on 23 January 1863 to Lieutenant-Colonel Fitzwygram, who had been second in command of the regiment in Colonel Shute's day. Fitzwygram was apparently an old friend of Dr Turnbull's and had himself fallen foul of the higher command several years earlier.

At the time of the troubles in the officers' mess and the early closing imposed by the divisional commander, Fitzwygram had written a letter to the general protesting at this restriction.

This was regarded as an aggravation of the situation and Colonel Fitzwygram was reprimanded. No doubt he was a ready sympathiser with Turnbull and Smales in their conflict with Crawley, to whom Fitzwygram had, as temporary commander, handed over the regiment in 1862.

However this may have been, he received Dr Turnbull's confidence in the form of this letter, which continued:

'I wish I could have placed this on paper and on official record, but the arbitrary government we live under out here prevents my doing so. In my addenda to Sergeant-Major Lilley's case I fear I have not expressed myself clearly.

'I do not mean to say that Dr Barnett and I had found Colonel Crawley's statement about the consumption of liquor to a large extent by Lilley to be correct, but that Mrs Lilley said that he was in the habit of taking a fair quantity daily, but she could give no definite idea of the quantity.

'I believe the acting adjutant [Davies] must have frightened the poor woman to make some admission, or perhaps it was merely trumped up by Davies and the Parsee that Lilley got the quantity stated . . .'

There is clearly in this letter an implied wish that Turnbull's second report should be known unofficially to be modified, and so to reduce any benefit that the addenda might be to Colonel Crawley.

The letter, or a copy of it, was actually forwarded to the Horse Guards by Captain Smales; what is not clear is how he came to be in possession of it. It is possible that Dr Turnbull sent him a copy, or perhaps Colonel Fitzwygram forwarded the original to Smales to make what use he could of it.

For in the weeks preceding the court martial of Colonel Crawley Smales was busy in London, discussing the case with friends who were to be prosecution witnesses—among them Colonel Fitzwygram, who was to speak as to Lilley's general character and sobriety.

Smales, of course, would have needed no telling that the place to send this letter was Whitehall.

The letter concluded, although again this part was not published in *The Times*:

'Every one of the sentries who were placed over him day and night, and who were examined by Colonel Crawley, stated that they had never seen him in the least intoxicated, or seen brandy taken into the room.'

This was not true, since the evidence of the sentries survives; and although none said that Lilley was ever intoxicated several testified as to his drinking brandy and offering it to them.

Dr Turnbull's letter concluded:

'Colonel Crawley stated to me in the Orderly Room that he was aware from the day he joined that Lilley was a sot. I remarked that if he thought that, it was strange that he should have entrusted him with the charge of the wines etc. in both the officers' and sergeants' mess, that I had always considered him a most sober man, and respected by everyone in the regiment.

'We who have spoken the truth feel as if we stood over a volcano.'

Captain Smales is the most likely one to have let Mr Samuel Lilley have a copy of the letter, but there is no surviving evidence that he did.

It was natural for him to view the colonel's impending ordeal with some satisfaction, and he was not a man to stay his hand if he could stir up additional trouble for his erstwhile tormentor.

Colonel Crawley's counsel in the forthcoming trial was to be Mr W. V. Harcourt;* his solicitor was Mr Alfred Richard Cocker.

In the last days before the court martial began Mr Harcourt raised with Mr Cocker the problem set by the custom of allowing military prisoners to have legal advice, but not allowing lawyers actually to speak in court on behalf of their clients.

He wrote: 'This practice is no doubt a remnant of the old barbarous usage by which, in all the courts, prisoners in criminal cases were denied the assistance of counsel. The

* Later Sir William Vernon Harcourt, Solicitor-General and Home Secretary.

humanity and good sense of later times has conceded to prisoners in all other criminal courts the avowed and unfettered aid of professional advisers. . . .

'I can conceive no possible reason why the methods which have been found by experience the best adapted for the elucidation of truth in the case of the rest of Her Majesty's subjects should not be equally applicable to prisoners arraigned before military tribunals. . . .

'In the approaching prosecution of Colonel Crawley the very system of courts martial itself will be on its trial. This would therefore seem a most appropriate occasion for putting that system on a satisfactory footing; and if the introduction of a new rule on this subject should be—as I think it should—desirable, no opportunity for such an alteration would appear more appropriate. . . . This application, of course, will not be regarded in the light of a particular favour to Colonel Crawley but as the introduction of a system for the regulation of courts martial in accordance with the practice of the ordinary criminal courts.'

If Mr Harcourt thought he would get away with a request of this nature with the naive assumption that it would 'not be regarded in the light of a particular favour to Colonel Crawley' he must have been remarkably innocent of the normal public reaction to be expected in such a circumstance.

It is inconceivable that an experienced lawyer could be so naive, and his letter must therefore be regarded as a formal and disingenuous attempt to win for himself the freedom to speak for his client.

The reply from the Duke of Cambridge was inevitable. He refused the application because 'it would be extremely injudicious at the present moment to make any alteration in the usual course which has been hitherto observed for the examination of witnesses before a General Court Martial.'

Colonel Crawley was to have, ostensibly, precisely the same sort of trial as Captain Smales had had. Justice, in the case of the notorious Colonel Crawley, was not only going to be done, but was manifestly going to be seen to be done.

13

A colonel on trial

THE court martial of Lieutenant-Colonel T. R. Crawley, which had been awaited with growing interest and eagerness by the whole country, began at Aldershot on 17 November 1863 under the presidency of Lieutenant-General Sir George Augustus Wetherall.

The trial took place in the Royal Aldershot Club House—The Club—in Farnborough Road. This building, although it has been altered during the last hundred years, still stands at Aldershot and is still the officers' club.

It was built in 1858 and contained rooms for reading, fencing, billiards, cards, and smoking. It was described by a writer in the 1850's as 'a rendezvous of all the choice spirits of the camp, where politics and matters connected with the turf are discussed with equal energy and gusto: where all grave questions, such as "What do you intend to do with yourself tomorrow, old fellah?" are debated and settled'.

The club was chosen because its chandelier-hung ballroom, with smaller rooms leading off it, was the most suitable accommodation near to the camp for a trial that was to engage scores of witnesses, lawyers, newspaper reporters, and an expected large crowd of spectators.

The main room of today's Officers' Club at Aldershot occupies roughly the same position as the old 'large room' where Colonel Crawley's trial was held.

The court consisted of four major-generals, four colonels and six lieutenant-colonels. The prosecutor was Colonel Sir Alfred Horsford, who was advised by the deputy Judge Advocate, Mr Denison.

Shortly before 11 a.m. the scene was set, except for the entrance of the principal character, Colonel Crawley.

A long table was provided for the members of the court in the centre of the room, with two smaller tables for the prosecutor and his advisers, and for Colonel Crawley and his lawyers. A wooden barrier separated the central court area from the public, so that the picture was one of the court and its servants in the centre of the ballroom, with a public area at either end of it.

At one end the spectators, consisting almost entirely of military men, stood to watch the proceedings. The other public area was reserved for high-ranking officers, important—or merely influential—civilians of both sexes for whom seats were provided.

The Times reporter describes the opening moments of the trial:

'Shortly before 11 a.m. the officers and men of the 6th Inniskilling Dragoons, who have been brought from India as witnesses in the case, were marched into the body of the court and presented a very imposing appearance. Had the authorities selected the representatives of that regiment on the score of personal appearance, or evident attention to drill, instead of their supposed capacity as witnesses they could hardly have brought together a finer body of men.'

The witnesses stood to attention while the members of the court answered their names, and were then marched out again.

At precisely 11 a.m. Colonel Crawley entered the court with his brother, Colonel Henry Crawley, and his lawyers. They bowed to the president and retired to the table prepared for them.

Although the prosecutor and Colonel Crawley were the only persons allowed to act as advocates in the trial, the legal battle was really conducted by the lawyers who primed their respective spokesmen with questions, objections, and sat beside them ever ready with the whispered word of advice or warning at dangerous moments.

After a preliminary skirmish in the form of a legal objection by Colonel Crawley which was turned down by the court, Sir Alfred Horsford opened the case for the prosecution.

He was a distinguished soldier, a colonel in the Rifle Brigade, and he made an impressive figure in his dark green uniform, his breast bright with the medals of twelve years' campaigning. The Kaffir War of 1847–8, the Crimea, the Mutiny, all were symbolised in coloured ribbons and glistening, chinking metal.

Colonel Horsford outlined the course the prosecution was to take.

'That part of the issue which is comprised in the words "great and grievous hardships and sufferings" involves several considerations, and will be supported by several distinct kinds of proof,' he said. 'Your attention will first be directed to what may be termed the more physical incidents of the case. And with reference to this there will be produced before you models of the buildings in which the sergeant-major was confined; and you will be enabled to judge how far the place of confinement, the position of the sentry, and the other local incidents of the confinement tended to produce the hardships and sufferings in question.'

Next, the court would be told of the constitution and habits of Sergeant-Major Lilley, and of the state of his wife's health at the time, so that they could judge how such a man in such a position was likely to be affected by such confinement.

Thirdly, they would have to consider the medical evidence.

'This will comprise generally the evidence respecting the hardships and sufferings sustained by Sergeant-Major Lilley and his wife, and will enable you to determine whether these hardships and sufferings were great and grievous.'

Then the court would have to decide whether these hardships and sufferings were caused by the unnecessary and undue severity with which the order for the close arrest was carried out.

'It has to be borne in mind,' said Colonel Horsford, 'that the prisoner received an order from the Commander-in-Chief at Bombay to keep Sergeant-Major Lilley in close arrest until the trial of Paymaster Smales was finally adjourned, and for the purpose of this trial that order may be regarded as legal.

'Therefore, for the mere keeping of the sergeant-major in close arrest, so long as the order was in force Lieutenant-Colonel Crawley cannot be held responsible.

'But the length of time during which the imprisonment actually lasted, and the indefinite duration which was assigned to it by the order, appear to me to become matters for your consideration and to have a bearing on the first charge when it is remembered that as the confinement was to be uncertain in its duration it ought to have been made—by the officer entrusted with its execution—as little grievous as possible from its very commencement.

'And as the course of events seemed to be rendering the confinement one of a more protracted character than could have been intended by the Commander-in-Chief, it will be for you to consider whether some steps ought not to have been taken, either to ascertain whether any definite limit was intended to be assigned to it, or to represent to the authority who gave the order that the duration of the confinement seemed to be becoming greater than he could have intended it to be. . . .'

One of the early witnesses on the first day of the trial was Sergeant Edward Mills. His evidence, as one of the commanders of the guard over Lilley, went to prove the strict nature of the watch; but some old personal animosity flared up when the prosecutor asked:

'What sort of man was Sergeant-Major Lilley, and what were his habits?'

'He consumed a great deal of liquor,' said Sergeant Mills. 'He drank very heavy, and could carry a great deal. I should describe him as a great, coarse, ignorant man.'

'Have you ever seen him drunk?'

'I have, very often.'

'Did you ever see him drunk on duty?'

'No, never.'

'Was he a man of active, stirring habits?'

'He rode about a great deal on a pony, but he could not walk, for he had bad feet. . . .'

'What were the orders of the sentry posted on the sergeant-major?'

'To keep his post till properly relieved by a non-commissioned officer of the guard: on no account to lose sight of his prisoner except when he went to the water closet.'

The president of the court wanted to know more about Lilley's alleged drunkenness:

'You have stated that you had many a time seen Sergeant-

Major Lilley drunk: specify the particular occasions alluded to.'

'In the first place it was in the year 1844 at Mr Daniels, the Three Crowns in Parliament Street, Nottingham. I assisted to carry him in. I saw him drunk again at Mr Williams', the Victoria, at Newcastle-on-Tyne.

'I saw him again drunk at Balaklava: he was in company with Sergeant-Major Moreton. He sent me down for three bottles of gin and gave me a sovereign to pay for them. I saw him drunk on Christmas Day at Scutari. I pulled off his boots and covered him up in bed that night.

'I saw him drunk at Durham when he was on recruiting service when the squadron lay there. I found him in his bed drunk.

'I also saw him drunk in the female hospital which he occupied when we first marched into Mhow: he lived there. The day we marched into Mhow I was regimental orderly sergeant. I went up to my tea at seven o'clock and he ordered me away like a dog. He was then drunk and I went away without anything. At Burhampore I saw him drunk in his tent on the line of march.'

'Did you report him as being drunk the day you were orderly sergeant and you say you saw him drunk?'

'I did not.'

Sergeant Mills clearly had old scores to settle with John Lilley. It is possible that the court had some misgivings as to the accuracy of his evidence, for the president's last question was:

'Did anyone else to your knowledge see him drunk on those occasions?'

'Not to my knowledge.'

The first prosecution witness to speak of the circumstances of Sergeant-Major Lilley's confinement was Lieutenant Thomas Joseph Fitzsimon, the former adjutant, now aged thirty-one.

He told of the events leading up to the arrest of the three sergeant-majors, and how the severity of Lilley's confinement was increased by the colonel's direct order that the sentries were not to lose sight of him 'night or day'.

In reply to further questions he said that he submitted a

written order to Colonel Crawley for the posting of sentries over the three men. The colonel 'added one or two words to it in his own handwriting'. Fitzsimon had given the order to Sergeant-Major Cotton who was to post the sentries, but he no longer had a copy of these orders.

He had been unwell about this time and Cornet Snell had taken over as Acting Adjutant on 4 or 5 May. Fitzsimon said he had resumed duty on 16 May and was suspended from the adjutancy on 22 May. These dates had some significance for Fitzsimon was not actually carrying out his duties as adjutant on the day Sergeant-Major Lilley complained to the court martial of the indignity caused to his wife by the sentries' presence.

The lieutenant also outlined the incident of his letter of complaint which he withdrew after the interviews with Colonel Crawley and Major-General Farrell.

This, of course, was vital to the second charge against Crawley—that he had falsely blamed the adjutant, Fitzsimon, for the way in which Lilley and his wife had been treated.

It was now time for Colonel Crawley to cross-examine Lieutenant Fitzsimon: but instead of following the usual course and beginning his cross-examination immediately, he asked for, and was given, permission to postpone it until the following day.

He made the request in a general way so that it would apply to all witnesses. The reason for his request, although he did not say so, was so that he could confer with his legal advisers at leisure and compile questions. It was a considerable favour which the court extended to him in this way, and made the construction of cross-examination an easier task for his lawyers compared with the more spontaneous effort of mind required in the ordinary way of court procedure.

For the sake of continuity cross-examination will be dealt with in this account as if it had occurred immediately following examination-in-chief.

Colonel Crawley was calling very few witnesses of his own and his case would therefore stand or fall on the extent to which he could dismantle the evidence given for the prosecution.

'In your opinion,' he asked Lieutenant Fitzsimon, 'were the quarters in which Lilley was confined comfortable or uncomfortable?'

'The first quarters, I think, were comfortable. The second quarters, in which he died, were not comfortable, especially for a married man.'

'Are these quarters as good as married men of the Inniskilling Dragoons inhabit now?'

'I think they are about the same.'

'Could they properly be called a bomb-proof oven? Is that a true or false description?'

'What I recollect of the second quarter, it was a bomb-proof building, though I never took particular notice.'

'Could they be called unfit for human habitation? Is that true or false?'

'It is not a true description; they are not unfit.'

This nibbled a little at the description given in parliament that Lilley's quarters were former stables, unfit for human beings to live in. From such small bricks is a defence built up. These things were admitted to be untrue by a witness who could not be described as friendly to the colonel.

'How came you to cease to be adjutant of the Inniskilling Dragoons?'

'I was suspended from the adjutancy in consequence of my commanding officer having reported me for having partaken of the paymaster's hospitality, and also because he stated I was incompetent to perform the duties of adjutant.'

The court could now have little doubt that Lieutenant Fitzsimon would not willingly assist Colonel Crawley. It had the effect of making anything that he did say in the colonel's favour more significant.

'Do you regard the adjutant of a regiment as a confidential and right-hand man of his commanding officer?' asked Crawley.

'Decidedly.'

'Do you think it consistent with the duty of a person in such a position to be living on terms of intimacy with a person standing in such relation to me as Mr Smales did?'

'I consider that having known Captain Smales and his family

for a long time—since they came to the regiment—and having always been on terms of intimacy with them, that I was not wrong in partaking of their hospitality.'

Colonel Crawley was meticulous in referring to his old enemy, Smales, as 'Mr'. The fact that he was by now on half-pay and pardoned was something that he chose not to recognise. To the colonel he was still a cashiered officer bereft of military title. The antagonism of Fitzsimon is shown in his equally careful restoration of Smales' rank in his replies.

The colonel had gone some way towards establishing that Fitzsimon was an unwilling witness: now he went on to the next stage, to attack his reliability on matters adverse to the colonel's case.

'Were you censured by the court martial at Mhow for the evasive character of your evidence?'

'I was censured by the Commander-in-Chief, Sir Hugh Rose,' came the reply.

'That is not the question. Were you censured by the court martial?'

'I do not recollect. . . . To the best of my recollection, when the remarks of the court martial were made I was away on leave. On my return, when I saw the remarks of the Commander-in-Chief it was the only thing I paid attention to.'

It had now been drawn to the court's attention that Lieutenant Fitzsimon had been found to be evasive when he was a witness at Mhow. That seed having been sown in the court's minds, it was germinated by the next few questions in a way that the prosecution could not have foreseen. The lieutenant's evasiveness was clearly demonstrated.

'In your opinion then, the first order given to you on 26 April was not one which was calculated to cause annoyance to Sergeant-Major Lilley?'

'I cannot state whether it was *calculated* to give annoyance or not,' replied Fitzsimon. 'The manner in which the sentry was posted could not have annoyed the sergeant-major.'

'If the sentries were posted according to the orders you received, and the manner in which the sentries were posted could cause no annoyance to Sergeant-Major Lilley, will you now answer the question that has already been put to you—

whether the first orders you received were calculated to cause annoyance to Sergeant-Major Lilley?'

Colonel Crawley in using the word 'calculated' was, of course, simply making use of a fairly common colloquialism. He might simply have said 'would cause' instead of 'calculated to cause'. But Lieutenant Fitzsimon chose to adopt its literal and more sinister meaning.

'If the meaning of the words "calculated to annoy" is whether the commanding officer *wished* thereby to annoy, I cannot say.'

'Do you think it possible that if the orders you first received were properly carried out by you, and did cause no annoyance to Sergeant-Major Lilley, still it might have been the *intention* of the commanding officer to annoy Sergeant-Major Lilley by those orders?'

'I cannot say. The commanding officer was very much enraged with him.'

'Do you consider that at the time I gave that order I had any desire to annoy Sergeant-Major Lilley in the matter of posting the sentries?'

'I should say not,' answered Fitzsimon.

At last, a grudging concession from the lieutenant that Crawley had not deliberately framed his orders for close arrest to satisfy any personal animosity towards Lilley.

The reluctance of the lieutenant could only have made a poor impression on the court, and at this stage of the proceedings it was not so much what Fitzsimon had said, as the way he said it.

He had clearly demonstrated his antagonism towards the colonel, and however much that attitude may have been justified by past events still it remained a fact which lessened the impact of anything the lieutenant said.

'Were your instructions to prevent their communicating with anyone outside?' asked Crawley.

The lieutenant agreed.

'Was it not the duty of the adjutant in the case of so serious an arrest to visit the first sentry who was posted?'

'In my opinion,' said Lieutenant Fitzsimon, 'it was the duty of the adjutant to visit the sentry as soon as he had time to do so, if he was not in any other way officially occupied.'

With these and many other similar questions Crawley established that Fitzsimon had not actually seen the sentries posted himself, and that he might therefore have been lax in carrying out his duties.

'Do you consider that one of the hardships of Sergeant-Major Lilley's arrest was a delay in giving the order for him to take exercise?' asked the colonel.

'No, I think the commanding officer ordered that he was to take exercise on its being notified to him that he required it.'

'If the desirableness of such exercise had been brought to my notice earlier by you or any other person, do you believe I should have given the order earlier?'

'If it had been brought to notice by me, I cannot say: but if it had been brought to the notice of the commanding officer by the medical officer I should say he would.'

'During the time you were adjutant did you ever request any indulgence for Sergeant-Major Lilley which was refused by me?'

'No. I do not recollect ever having requested any indulgence for him whatsoever.'

Employing a common legal tactic, Colonel Crawley began to examine the lieutenant on details in an attempt to shake his testimony.

'Who was the first sentry you saw, and where did you find him posted?'

'I do not recollect who he was. The first time I recollect visiting the sentry in the first quarters in which the sergeant-major was confined he came to the back door to me. . . .'

The colonel pressed the question again, demanding 'a plain answer' . . . Where was the first sentry posted?

'He was posted inside the quarters: he could not have been posted in any particular spot as his orders were not to lose sight of the sergeant-major day or night, and consequently he was obliged to follow him from one room to another.'

It was essential for the colonel to discredit the lieutenant's evidence, for the *way* in which the order for close arrest had been carried out was the crux of the case against him. But so far he had little success with the former adjutant who was no doubt enjoying a revenge that had sweetened with the passing of time. But Crawley had to persevere.

'It has been stated in parliament that Mrs Lilley was compelled to perform all the functions of nature in the presence of the sentries: to your knowledge is that statement true or false?'

'I do not know.'

'Did you ever yourself receive any report of such annoyance or inconvenience from Sergeant-Major or Mrs Lilley, or from anyone else?'

'I never to my recollection received a report from Sergeant-Major Lilley or from anyone else; I have heard it spoken of.'

This was more than the colonel required or desired in the reply. He immediately objected to the last six words as hearsay. The prosecutor—cool, unemotional, uninvolved in the proceedings except as a matter of disagreeable duty—insisted that the reply should stand as it had been given.

Crawley—quick-tempered, emotionally involved and with everything at stake—replied warmly:

'I must protest against the acceptance of hearsay evidence foisted gratuitously into the answer by the witness. I beg that this part of the answer be expunged, or my protest recorded in the proceedings.'

Captain Smales, a spectator to the scene, may have smiled wryly at the recollection of his own numerous protests at Mhow, and his own insistence on their being recorded when turned down by the court.

The president ruled that the answer ought to remain as it had been given. The colonel returned to the task in hand without further argument.

'You have stated that the sentries were ordered not to intrude on Sergeant-Major Lilley when he went to the rear: who gave this order?'

'To the best of my recollection it was given by my commanding officer.'

'Now, Mr Fitzsimon,' said Crawley, 'I must ask you for a straightforward answer to this question: do you intend to convey to the court the impression that whilst I was careful to protect the privacy of *Sergeant-Major* Lilley, I intended that of *Mrs* Lilley to be intruded upon?'

'I really cannot say what my commanding officer intended,' came the reply that even down the years retains a suggestion of the sardonic tones in which it seems to have been given.

Colonel Crawley now turned to the second charge against him—that of unjustly blaming Lieutenant Fitzsimon for the Lilley tragedy when he addressed the court at Mhow.

'Why did you abstain from taking any notice of my speech from June to November?'

'I was not aware of the colonel's speech until I came back from leave of absence. I had been up country at Lucknow, and was part of that time sick.'

'Is it usual for an officer who has made a serious charge against another officer, and upon consideration and reflection has withdrawn it, to revive and reproduce that charge at a later period?'

The lieutenant was not to be put off by the implied lack of gentlemanly instincts.

'It may not be usual,' he said. 'I withdrew that letter at the time only in consequence of its having been pronounced insubordinate by the major-general, and as he considered it might produce my professional ruin.'

'Having withdrawn that letter, when did you first think of renewing the charges against me?' asked Colonel Crawley.

'I am not exactly aware that I renewed the charges until they were called for from me by the Horse Guards. On my return from India to this country on sick leave I requested that the medical board before which I was to appear would also make an examination of my eyesight in consequence of the allegation that had been made against me by my commanding officer.'

The president took up the questioning of the lieutenant, who may have been wondering by now whether it was he himself who was on trial. He was again asked whether he considered it was his duty as adjutant to see the sentries posted.

'I consider it was my duty to see the place where the sentries were posted, but I do not consider it my duty to post the sentries myself.'

'If you saw the sentry on his post, describe the position of the post.'

'In the first bungalow I went to the back door of room No

4* and he came to the door. I did not see the post in the first bungalow. When I went to visit the sentry he frequently came and opened the door for me himself.'

'You have already stated that you *do* consider it was your duty to see the place where the sentry was posted: so you now acknowledge that you failed in your duty in this point; is this so?'

'So far as not going in to see him on his post, I did.'

'Did you ever take any measures to prevent any improper interference with Mrs Lilley by the sentry?'

'No, I never gave any orders except those which I received from my commanding officer.'

'Did you consider that you had any discretion as to the posting of the sentries?'

'No, there was no discretionary power given me.'

The president's probing came to an end, and Colonel Crawley had the right of further questioning.

'What were the orders given you which you say left you no discretion as to the post of the sentry?' he asked.

'That the sentries were not to lose sight of the prisoner night or day.'

'If there had been a particular position in the house which would have enabled the sentry to keep sight of the prisoner night and day, would that have been in compliance with your orders?'

'Yes.'

'How could you tell whether there was such a position or not without going into the house to examine it?'

'I could not tell.'

Lieutenant Fitzsimon was obviously drained now of resistance to the questions that revealed him as an inefficient officer or, at least, an inefficient adjutant. But, it will be recalled, he had had limited experience of this key disciplinary post. His confession of some inadequacy under the questioning of this array of senior officers did not alter the fact that the order not to lose sight of Lilley day or night, and for the sentry to be posted inside the house without any qualifying instructions as to intrusion on privacy, had come directly and in a forceful

* Servant's room. See p. 43.

and peremptory manner from Lieutenant-Colonel Crawley.

Despite this, Lieutenant Fitzsimon must have been feeling somewhat in the position of a scapegoat on the question of the annoyance to Mrs Lilley.

Colonel Crawley had no further questions and the lieutenant withdrew. Crawley had not gained much from him on the first charge; but on the second charge, with the help of the court, Fitzsimon had acknowledged some responsibility for the positioning of the sentries and the consequential annoyance to Mrs Lilley for which the colonel had publicly blamed him.

It was a start in constructing the edifice of defence.

14

Release came too late

MAJOR James Hyde Champion was the Assistant Adjutant General to the Mhow Division of the Bombay army. He was responsible, among other things, for the quartering of the army and was, naturally, familiar with the barracks at Mhow.

He was called to prove the dimensions and construction of the Lilleys' last two homes that were the subject of so much notoriety.

His evidence for the prosecution was formal and need not be presented in detail; but Colonel Crawley had some important questions to put to him in cross-examination.

'What,' he asked, 'is your opinion as to the first bungalow in respect of its accommodation?'

'That it is very full and ample, far larger than is usually allotted to sergeants in India.'

'Had Sergeant-Major Lilley and his wife, during his confinement in the first bungalow, free access to five rooms and a verandah?'

'To the best of my belief he had.'

'Was the first place of Lilley's confinement a bomb-proof building formerly used as stables which had since been pulled down as unfit for the occupation of troops, and is that an accurate description of the first bungalow?'

'No, it is not.'

'Was the place in which Lilley was confined more like an oven than a human habitation: is that a true state of things?'

'No, it is not a true account of the state of things.'

'Was the first bungalow like a black hole of Calcutta, or the hold of a slave ship: is that true?'

'No, it is not.'

Here, for the first time, was a reply on oath by a person of authority and standing who was personally familiar with the background to the Lilley scandal. So far as the first bungalow was concerned it utterly disposed of the lurid descriptions given in parliament and press.

Colonel Crawley now began to examine the conditions in the bungalow in more detail. Major Champion produced correspondence which showed that Crawley had tried to get reasonable alternative accommodation for Lilley before removing him from his original spacious quarters.

He naturally laid considerable emphasis on his efforts in this respect. In the case of one alternative residence that had been suggested the colonel had apparently asked that the roof be chuppered, a term meaning that hay was spread on a roof to insulate it to some extent from the worst heat of the sun.

'Does it appear to you that I exhibited a spirit of malice or desire to act oppressively towards Sergeant-Major Lilley?' asked the colonel.

'Most decidedly not.'

From Major Champion the court learned that Colonel Crawley had written to him on 24 May 1862, the eve of Lilley's death, asking if the three sergeant-majors might be released from close arrest.

The major had replied the following day to the effect that the Mhow commander, Major-General Farrell, authorised their release from close arrest to simple arrest, which would have given them freedom within the limits of the camp area: but by the time this note was delivered—by the time it was being written even—Regimental Sergeant-Major John Lilley was dead.

Major Champion said that Colonel Crawley was the first person to suggest the relaxation of the arrest of the three sergeant-majors, with the exception of Major-General Farrell who had several times spoken of his regret that he could not go against the order from Bombay that they were to remain in close arrest until the end of Captain Smales' court martial.

'On the release of the sergeant-majors did General Farrell make an address to the surviving sergeants?'

'Yes . . . in the presence of the officers and non-commissioned officers of the regiment.'

The address was then read out in court. It was a portentous lecture, heavy with military admonishments and moral warnings, and 'the consolation of forgiveness'. The fact that the two surviving sergeant-majors had apparently been publicly forgiven for something they had never been charged with, much less tried for, may have struck those assembled as being rather strange.

When the court had heard the speech Colonel Crawley concluded his cross-examination with two important questions. It will be remembered that Mr Fortescue, in revealing the story of the Mhow court martial in the House of Commons, had said that when the two surviving sergeant-majors were released one of them had been 'a raving lunatic' and was taken to hospital 'suffering from brain fever'.

The date of their release was 25 May 1862, some twelve hours after Lilley died, and Major-General Farrell's speech was read on 6 June.

The colonel asked: 'Do I understand you to say that Sergeant-Major Wakefield was well enough to be present on 6 June at the reading of that address?'

'He was present on that occasion and in apparent perfect health.'

'Did he seem to you at that time to be a raving maniac?'

'He did not.'

The evidence of Troop Sergeant-Major Cotton was important not only for what he said, but for the fact that it was in no way challenged by Colonel Crawley in cross-examination.

Mr Cotton told the court:

'Colonel Crawley ordered me to go and see that the sentries were properly posted: that is, inside the quarters.'

Since Crawley made no attempt to shake this evidence it was an admission that he had, in fact, ordered the sentries to keep Lilley in sight at all times inside his house.

Much of the testimony in a trial has, necessarily, to be repetitive. What may be said by one witness, acquires greater force if repeated by another. It is not necessary to go through the orderly room scene* which had also been described by Lieutenant Fitzsimon, at which Sergeant-Major Cotton received his order to alter the sentry post. There can be no doubt that Crawley did lose his temper and did make strong and insensitive remarks about the Lilleys and their plight.

Major Swindley went through the scene again in detail and, it appears, with some relish in condemning Crawley.

Through Major Swindley the prosecutor recalled another incident which showed the colonel's obsessive feeling about keeping Lilley incommunicado.

'During the course of the court martial at Mhow do you recollect anything occurring about a man named Little?'

'I do,' said Swindley. 'I received an order to attend the orderly room to deal with the prisoners. Private Little was brought before me charged with having allowed communication to take place between Mrs Gibson, a woman of the regiment, and Sergeant-Major Lilley.

'I examined him as to the charge, found that it was not supported by the evidence adduced, and I ordered the man's release, and the crime sheet to be torn up so that nothing should be recorded against him. The crime sheet was torn up by the adjutant.

'On the following morning I was ordered to attend at the orderly room before Colonel Crawley, and was there reprimanded by him for my decision.

'The crime sheet was produced, the fragments of it having been sewn together. Colonel Crawley remarked that, from the evidence he had heard, he would have tried the man by court martial.'

'What was Mrs Gibson stated to have done?'

'Mrs Gibson was supposed to have communicated with Sergeant-Major Lilley.'

'What character did Sergeant-Major Lilley bear?'

'He bore the highest.'

That was the substance of Major Swindley's evidence for the prosecution. In view of the bad feeling between Swindley and Crawley the major would probably have been pleased to annoy the colonel by dismissing the charge against Private Little.

* See p. 42.

Colonel Crawley's cross-examination was clearly designed to suggest that Swindley was not a truthful witness and was actuated by malice.

'Did the court martial at Mhow think it necessary to remark on the strong animus you had displayed against me in giving your testimony?'

'The court did condemn me for having shown animus, but I disclaim that I showed any animus whatever at that court martial.'

'Have you never on any other occasion, Major Swindley, expressed and exhibited a strong feeling of hostility to me?'

'In private life I have; in public life never.'

'Did Sir Hugh Rose remark that in your evidence on the Mhow court martial you convicted yourself of having used towards your commanding officer in the orderly room insubordinate, disrespectful and defiant language?'

'Sir Hugh Rose does so remark.'

'Do you believe that the quarters in which Sergeant-Major and Mrs Lilley were lodged were unfit for human habitation?'

'I had never been inside the quarters where they were lodged, and therefore I cannot say. I have been in similar quarters. I should say, for married people shut up and confined in them, they were.'

'Are there no married families of the non-commissioned officers and soldiers of your regiment worse lodged than they were?'

'There are. There is a great difference between being shut up, and *living* in quarters. There are married families of the 6th Dragoons in similar quarters—I cannot say in worse.'

'When you state that Sergeant-Major Lilley was shut up, do you know that he had, in the first house, free access to five rooms and a verandah, and in the second quarter to two rooms and two verandahs, and that he had twice a day the exercise recommended by the doctor?'

'No I do not,' came the defiant reply, 'I do not know how many rooms Sergeant-Major Lilley's first house had. I had never been in the house, and I know nothing about it. To my recollection of my own sergeant-major's quarters there was only one room and an inner verandah . . . but I have never heard the inner verandah called a room before.'

Crawley turned to the question of exercise. Swindley had seen Lilley exercising on the parade ground: was that what he meant by being shut up?

Swindley's reply appears to have had overtones of contempt: 'He was undergoing confinement—imprisonment! That is to say he was marked as a prisoner every day during his exercise, with an armed sentry in the rear of him.'

'When you say an armed sentry, do you not know that Sergeant-Major Lilley was never accompanied by a private soldier, but always by a sergeant?'

'An armed sentry,' repeated Major Swindley with some warmth it seems. 'Well—a non-commissioned officer.' The hostility and disdain in which Swindley held Crawley is inherent in the phrasing of his replies.

'When you have heard this subject discussed in your presence,' continued Colonel Crawley, 'have you always taken care to state that the quarters in which Sergeant-Major Lilley died were similar to those occupied by your own sergeant-major?'

'I do not remember discussing the subject of the quarters at all, and I cannot answer the question.'

'Will you undertake to say that the subject of the inconvenience and unhealthiness of the quarters in which Sergeant-Major Lilley died has never been mentioned in your presence?'

'I will not undertake to say anything of the kind,' replied Swindley, coldly.

'Now I ask you to answer the question carefully. Will you undertake to say that you have never sought to give the impression to other people, and encouraged the belief in other persons, that Sergeant-Major and Mrs Lilley were, during the whole course of the arrest, shut up in one room?'

'If ever I did speak about it to other people I certainly should have done so,' said Major Swindley. 'Not during the whole course of the arrest, but during the latter part, as from the recollection of my own sergeant-major's quarters I believe them to have been shut up in one room.'

Swindley's evidence came to an end. He had tried to give the impression that the subject of Lilley's confinement had not been widely discussed in his presence. He could not bring himself to tell the direct lie that Lilley's quarters had never been mentioned to him; but that anyone as closely connected with the events as Major Swindley could not remember discussing something that had become the talk of the British Empire is difficult to believe. It must have been a major topic of conversation among Inniskillings of all ranks for many weeks.

This thought could not have escaped the members of the court, who not only saw and heard Swindley's evident antagonism towards Crawley, but may have wondered how much this emotional factor should count against their acceptance of what Swindley said in court.

15

Evidence of Dr Barnett

BEFORE calling the important evidence from the regimental doctors, Colonel Horsford dealt with the circumstances in which Lilley came to be housed in the second and fatal bungalow.

His witness was Quartermaster Charles Wooden, an early winner of the Victoria Cross, and a man whom he was later to describe as 'open as day and as honest as truth itself'.

Quartermaster Charles Wooden, V.C., told the court:

'The quarters occupied by Sergeant-Major Lilley and the quartermaster sergeant were ordered to be vacated, and these N.C.O.s to be removed into other quarters.

'There was a great want of room in barracks, and some correspondence was entered into to get more quarters for the 6th Dragoons. After some days a staff sergeant's quarters was given over to the regiment.

'This quarter was, as nearly as I can remember, about a quarter of a mile from barracks, and I suggested to Colonel Crawley that he put Sergeant-Major Lilley in that bungalow, remarking that as Sergeant-Major Lilley was under arrest he would not be wanted for any duty.

'Colonel Crawley asked me could I place him anywhere else? I replied: "I have no other place except the married men's quarters."

'Colonel Crawley replied: "Neither will do. The one is too far, the other is too open, and Lilley will be up to some more tricks."

'The colonel directed me then to give that staff sergeant's quarter to the quartermaster-sergeant, and to remove the sergeant-major of H Troop, and to place Sergeant-Major Lilley in the troop sergeant-major's quarter.

'I remarked to the colonel that the quarters were very small.

'The colonel said: "The quarters are good enough for one sergeant and are good enough for another."

'I remarked: "But as the troop sergeant-major is a single man . . ."

'The colonel got rather impatient and said: "I don't want any more buts; do as I tell you." I then gave orders for the troop sergeant-major to vacate the bungalow where he was, and to put Sergeant-Major Lilley into it.'

'What character did Sergeant-Major Lilley bear?'

'A very good N.C.O. and soldier.'

'What character as to sobriety?'

'A very sober, steady man.'

This evidence, containing a characteristic cameo of the way Colonel Crawley dealt with his subordinates and his brushing aside entirely the fact that he was putting a married couple into the small quarters allotted to a single man, was not shaken in the few questions Crawley put in cross-examination.

The brief testimony of Private James Reynolds, elicited in cross-examination by Colonel Crawley, had more significance than was at first apparent.

'Do you remember being present when I remarked upon the sentry over Sergeant-Major Lilley's house being out in the sun about mid-day, and my ordering Lieutenant Fitzsimon to place the sentry inside under cover?'

'I remember the occasion,' Private Reynolds replied.

'Was that shortly after the arrest of Sergeant-Major Lilley?'

'Yes, within six or seven days of his arrest.'

There was little else of any consequence in Private Reynold's evidence; but it showed that at the beginning of the arrest Colonel Crawley saw nothing wrong, so far as carrying out his orders was concerned, in the sentry's being *outside* the house. There was no suggestion that he ought to have been inside the sergeant-major's quarters; only a suggestion of thoughtfulness on the colonel's part that the mid-day sun might be harmful to the sentry.

The evidence of Sergeant Eleazar Eyland was not challenged by Colonel Crawley, yet it was of importance to the prosecution.

The prosecutor asked the sergeant, who had commanded the guard over Lilley on 27 April and 21 May:

'Do you recollect what orders you took over about the sentries?'

'Yes,' said Sergeant Eyland. 'On the first occasion my orders were that the sentry was to take charge of the prisoner; to allow no communication with anyone outside; and the native servant was to be searched on going in and coming out. Those were the orders on the evening of 27 April.

'On the morning of the 28th I received fresh orders from Sergeant-Major Cotton. They were to the effect that the sentry was to be placed in the sergeant-major's bungalow in his quarters. I accordingly placed the sentry in the bungalow myself.'

'What were the orders on 21 May?'

'Between 28 April and 21 May the sergeant-major had been shifted to another bungalow. The orders were simply the same as on the former occasion in the other bungalow, only that the sergeant-major had permission to sleep in the verandah and sit in the verandah.'

It will be remembered that three days after 28 April—on 1 May—Corporal Blake was arrested by Sergeant Mills because he had posted a sentry outside Lilley's quarters instead of inside. So that at this early stage of the arrest it was already of an oppressive nature, although the only reason for it, ostensibly, was that Colonel Crawley thought sentries ought not to be out in the mid-day sun.

The evidence of Mrs Ann Cotton, wife of Sergeant-Major Cotton, is worth recalling not for its value in the prosecution of Colonel Crawley, but for the additional detail it reveals of the last moments of John Lilley.

After describing how she was first called to the sick man's bungalow by Mrs Lilley, and her sending for the doctor, Mrs Cotton said:

'I stayed with him until about ten minutes to one. I then returned to my own quarters and remained about a quarter of an hour, when Mrs Lilley called to me again and said her husband was dying. I immediately went in and found him still worse. He looked at me very hard. Mrs Lilley said: "Do you know who that is?" He said: "Yes, it is Mrs Cotton."

'He then took my hand and said: "Mrs Cotton, I am dying."

'I said: "Don't say so, Lilley, you will soon be better."

'He said: "No, my child, I never shall." He took my hand again and said: "Goodbye, may God bless you."

'I then assisted Mrs Lilley from the bed where her husband was dying and laid her on a sofa until all was over. I then had her removed into my own quarters, where she remained until about a fortnight before her death.'

Colonel Crawley did not cross-examine Mrs Cotton. What was there to ask her? Her evidence came perhaps as a reminder to the court of what this trial was all about. Mrs Cotton, with her poignant recollections of Lilley's last words, brought vividly to mind again the sweaty, oil-lamp-lit horror of the sergeant-major's last hours.

It was also opportune that the court should have had this account of Lilley's death just before Assistant Surgeon Oliver Barnett was called to give evidence.

Dr Barnett does not figure as a particular partisan in the disagreement that brought notoriety to the officers' mess of the 6th Inniskilling Dragoons.

He was, by the nature of his duty, a friend of Dr Turnbull, and four years his junior, and it may be that he was to some extent influenced by Turnbull—if not through weakness then through expediency, for he had to work with the senior surgeon.

Dr Barnett told the court that Mrs Lilley had suffered from consumption and that her health was declining throughout her husband's arrest.

'Could the sentry see into Mrs Lilley's bedroom?' asked the prosecutor.

'From No 2 room he could see into No 3—Mrs Lilley's bedroom.* I should say not distinctly without removing the chick that was on the door.'

'Could you see through the chick?'

'Yes, I have frequently seen the sentry over the lining of the chick: the chick was lined half way up with a sort of red

* See p. 43.

cotton. I could see the sentry's head over that.'

'Could he hear anything that was going on in the bedroom?'

'The conversation carried on in the bedroom could be heard in the other room distinctly, unless it was in an undertone. In my visits to Mrs Lilley I always spoke to her in an undertone in asking her professional questions, lest it should be overheard by the sentry.'

The doctor explained that Mrs Lilley had to spend the greater part of each day in bed. Sometimes she felt better and could sit up; but often she was confined to bed all day.

Colonel Horsford asked Dr Barnett how he felt as a doctor about the position of the sentries.

'I consider it was an annoyance to the sergeant-major and his wife, who was then so seriously ill,' replied Dr Barnett.

'Did Colonel Crawley ever consult you as to the position of the sentry with reference to Mrs Lilley's convenience in either bungalow?'

'Never.'

'Do you remember the inconvenience to Mrs Lilley being rendered less at any time during the arrest from the alteration of the position of the sentry?'

'No, I do not.'

'What can you say of the quantity of brandy that Mrs Lilley used daily during the arrest?'

'Mrs Lilley used daily generally three or four glasses of brandy on my recommendation.'

'What is your opinion about the quantity of brandy that Mrs Lilley might have consumed daily without any injurious effect?'

'Considering the extreme debility in which Mrs Lilley was at the time, she might have consumed three or four, or perhaps four or five glasses of brandy daily without having any injurious effect.'

Dr Barnett said he had never seen any signs of drink in Lilley either before or after his arrest. Lilley had first been permitted to take exercise about 30 April and first had leave to sit out on the verandah of his bungalow during arrest 'at the latter end of May'.*

'Did you have any conversation with Colonel Crawley

* Lilley was arrested on 26 April.

about the quantity of brandy that Sergeant-Major Lilley is said to have consumed during his arrest?'

Dr Barnett replied:

'On the morning of 9 June, when riding towards the parade ground, I met Colonel Crawley at the corner of the road below the hospital. I rode with the colonel towards the parade, and he then remarked to me: "Have you any opinion how much brandy Lilley drank during his confinement?" I said: "No, I do not, because I never observed the slightest appearance of drink upon him during the time he was in confinement."

'Colonel Crawley then said he had 23 bottles of brandy, 12 pints of ale, a bottle of port wine, and some gin, I think. When the parade was dismissed I waited on Colonel Crawley and asked him if he wished me to make any addition to our report on the sergeant-major's case in reference to the quantity of liquor supplied to him during his arrest? The colonel replied: "No, I have done it, or I will do it in my report." '

Dr Barnett said that Lilley died of heat apoplexy and that being a very stout man made him more liable to this condition. He then formally produced the post mortem report on Lilley and the controversial opinion as to the cause of death.*

It was 4 p.m. and the end of the eighth day of the trial.

In cross-examination the following day Colonel Crawley's first purpose was to prove through the doctor that he was not the inhuman creature that the public believed him to be.

Dr Barnett agreed that before the arrest Mrs Crawley had regularly visited Mrs Lilley in her illness, for her death had long been expected.

'Do you remember that I gave Sergeant-Major Lilley leave to precede the regiment to Mhow on account of the death of one of his children and the illness of another?'

'I do.'

'Do you consider that I was at all aware that the close arrest of Sergeant-Major Lilley was inflicting, or likely to inflict, fatal injury on his health?'

No, the doctor did not think the colonel was aware of that. Dr Barnett agreed he had been a regular visitor to the Crawley

*See pages 65 and 67.

house to look after Mrs Crawley and her mother, who were both ill, but he had never made any representations to the colonel about Lilley or his wife or the consequences of the conditions of close arrest.

'Was the death of Sergeant-Major Lilley under the circumstances, in your judgment, an event which anyone could have anticipated?'

This was a question that the doctor could only agree with unless he wished to confess to gross incompetence; and, of course, in absolving himself he excused Crawley, the layman, for not foreseeing such a thing either.

'No one could have anticipated such an event,' he said. 'I never did.'

'How long before his death did you first observe his health had begun to be affected?'

'The sergeant-major was in his usual health the second day before his death; because he was one entire day ill and he died the morning of the next day.'

'Was any report made by you or anyone else to me of his indisposition until his death?'

No, no such report had been made. It was not usual to do so until the day after a man became ill.

Colonel Crawley now came to the question of Lilley's drinking habits, and asked what enquiries the doctors had made about them.

Dr Barnett replied:

'After my interview with Colonel Crawley on 9 June, I waited on Mrs Lilley in the course of the day and communicated to her what Colonel Crawley had told me in the morning, and asked her whether her husband had been in the habit of drinking a considerable quantity of brandy.'

The prosecutor objected to this evidence as 'the worst form of hearsay evidence'. They were hearing of a conversation with someone now dead about the character of someone else, also dead, and neither person could therefore be questioned about it.

After some legal argument Colonel Crawley turned instead to two medical-military books and quoted authorities on the effect of alcohol and its tendency to bring on heat apoplexy in tropical climates.

Dr Barnett agreed with the writers' conclusions.

Then, asked Crawley, did the doctor still stand by the addendum to the post mortem report and the opinion that drink did not substantially alter the course of Lilley's illness?

But Dr Barnett stood firm:

'It *modified* that report, but did not alter it substantially.'

That was to say that the drink may have had something to do with Lilley's death but the other factors, his imprisonment and enforced idleness, his wife's illness and general depression brought on by his circumstances were the principal causes of his death.

The prosecutor re-examined Dr Barnett concerning his visits to Colonel Crawley's home. Colonel Crawley had seemed to be suggesting that the subject of Lilley had never been mentioned by Dr Barnett because there had been nothing to complain about in his conditions of arrest.

'Had you any reasons for not alluding to the subject of the arrest while you were in attendance upon some sick members of Colonel Crawley's family?' he asked.

'Yes. There was a mutual silence observed between members of Colonel Crawley's family and myself on all subjects in connection with the proceedings then going on at Mhow. . . . These subjects were never mentioned by me in Colonel Crawley's house to any members of his family, or by them to me.'

'I considered it necessary for the strict discharge of my official duty to observe silence on these matters as much as possible. It was my wish to be on terms with all the officers of my regiment, and had I become a partisan of Colonel Crawley or of Paymaster Smales I do not think I should have succeeded in doing so.'

The president also had a few questions for the doctor.

'Are four or five glasses of brandy a day a usual medical comfort for a woman in consumption during the hot season at Mhow?'

'I consider that in the case of Mrs Lilley, who was suffering very extreme exhaustion, that four or five glasses of brandy was not a considerable quantity for her to take; and the great irritability of her stomach and bowels, from which she constantly suffered, did not admit of her taking solid food or nutritious broths.'

The questioning turned to the doctor's conversation with Colonel Crawley about the brandy apparently consumed by Lilley and the enquiries that had been made afterwards. Hearsay evidence or not, the court was interested to know what Mrs Lilley had had to say on the subject of her husband's drinking.

'State exactly, or as nearly as you can, all that passed between you and Mrs Lilley at that interview,' said the president.

'After my conversation with Colonel Crawley in the morning I waited on Mrs Lilley and asked her if the statement made to me by Colonel Crawley was true or not. She said her husband took some brandy and soda water, or brandy and water, every day. And she added: "But I do not think so much as to do him any harm. Do you think it did, sir?" I replied: "I hope not."'

'You, however, thought it had done so much harm that you added it as a predisposing cause of his death?' remarked the president pointedly.

'That was presuming he *had* taken a considerable quantity of brandy. I considered it necessary to add that to my report, it had been so emphatically stated by Colonel Crawley in the morning that he had consumed a large quantity.'

'Did Mrs Lilley tell you the quantity of brandy her husband drank daily?'

'No. She did not mention any definite quantity.'

'Is it the practice in the 6th Dragoons to frame medical reports upon the statement of the commanding officer?'

'No, it is not.'

With this sarcasm, implying that the doctor had allowed a not-entirely-confirmed lay opinion to influence his professional judgment, the court's questions and Dr Barnett's evidence came to an end.

He had told his story fairly, without apparent hostility towards Colonel Crawley. He had established the colonel's point that strong drink could prove fatal in the tropics in certain conditions and that Mrs Lilley had spoken of her husband's regular drinking habits.

Colonel Crawley could not, on the whole, have been displeased at the result on record from Dr Barnett's evidence.

16

Evidence of Dr Turnbull

IF THE evidence of Dr Barnett had been given with fairness and restraint, the same cannot be said of the testimony of his superior, the regimental surgeon, Dr Turnbull.

The long-standing enmity he felt towards Crawley, dating from the mess feud over Mrs Renshaw, is clear from his answers both to the questions of the prosecutor and of Colonel Crawley himself.

He told the prosecutor that Sergeant-Major Lilley was first allowed to take exercise after his arrest on 30 April; that is, four days after the arrest took place.

'What is your opinion of the effect, as regards health, of the manner in which that exercise was taken?'

'I consider that the good effect of that exercise was in a great measure nullified by the manner in which it was carried out.'

'Did you apply to Colonel Crawley for permission for Sergeant-Major Lilley to sit in the verandah?'

'On 18 May Assistant Surgeon Barnett reported to me that the prisoners felt their rooms very close and hot and wished the indulgence of being allowed to sit in the verandah.

'I went to the orderly room and reported this to Colonel Crawley. I had previously to this visited Sergeant-Major Lilley and ascertained from him what was the cause of the complaint . . . and I reported this to Colonel Crawley in the adjutant's presence.

'Colonel Crawley replied: "Why, the sergeant-majors have morning and evening exercise; what more do they require?" I repeated the request of Sergeant-Major Lilley and told Colonel Crawley that I had simply brought this to his notice, and that it was for him to act in the matter, or not, as he thought proper.'

From this recollection of the conversation it is apparent that, by his manner and phrasing, Dr Turnbull had made it perfectly clear that he was throwing the responsibility for the well-being of the arrested man entirely upon the colonel, and was making his own position clear in the matter. It is not unusual for a subordinate to make his responsibility, or lack of it, plain to the man in ultimate authority, and it very often has the effect that it did in the case of Colonel Crawley: he agreed to the doctor's request on behalf of the prisoners.

'Was there a coroner's inquest held about Sergeant-Major Lilley's death?'

'There was not.'

'Was it a case in which a coroner's inquest would ordinarily have been held?'

'I think so.'

There was apparently an innuendo here that Colonel Crawley ought, as commanding officer, to have ordered an inquest to be held.

'Will you now inform the court what is your present opinion as to the cause of Sergeant-Major Lilley's death?'

'The heat of that season of the year, the predisposition of the patient to congestion, the peculiar and painful circumstances of his position, the illness of his wife, the mental anxiety, the grief and depression of spirits he suffered during his confinement, together with the bilious and nervous derangement induced by a sedentary life in a man of the sergeant-major's active habits, all acted as exciting causes to produce the complaint of which he died. I wish to add that this opinion is to a certain extent modified by my subsequent report.'

Colonel Crawley intervened to point out that the doctor had been asked for his present opinion, not the opinion he held at the time.

However, the point was not taken up by the prosecutor and it may be assumed that Dr Turnbull's opinion as recorded at the time of Lilley's death, and to a great extent repeated when he made the above reply, was unchanged.

There was a noticeable tension, a tangible antagonism between the two men when Colonel Crawley began his cross-examination of the doctor. Dr Turnbull had made it very clear in his replies to the prosecutor that he was not there to assist

Crawley in any way, and if he could give his testimony against him an additional damaging twist he was only too willing to do so.

Colonel Crawley went straight into the attack:

'In your opinion is part of the duty of a regimental surgeon to ascertain whether a soldier of a plethoric habit and under close arrest in the hot weather in India does, or does not, consume a considerable quantity of brandy daily?'

'If he has reason to suppose that the prisoner is addicted to the use of spirits, I think it is the duty of the medical officer who attends upon him to find out whether he does consume a considerable quantity of spirits daily or not.'

Dr Turnbull had simply returned the question in the form of an answer with the all-important proviso 'if he has reason to' think the man has been drinking. According to witness after witness, Lilley had been a man of temperate habit. And yet there was the unchallengeable evidence of his wife.

'How often did you visit Sergeant-Major Lilley during the course of his arrest for the purpose of making a medical inspection of his health?'

'I never visited R.S.M. Lilley for the purpose of prescribing for him: I have seen him frequently during the period of his arrest; it was the duty of Assistant Surgeon Barnett to see the prisoner daily.'

'Did you anticipate Sergeant-Major Lilley's death as a probable consequence of the arrest under which he was placed?'

'No, I did not anticipate that.'

'After you had sent in your first report to me on the case of Sergeant-Major Lilley, did I not on 9 June call your attention to the quantity of spirituous liquor Lilley was supposed to have consumed during his arrest, and did I not then ask you whether you chose to make any enquiries on the subject, and whether you would wish to make any alterations in your report?'

'Yes, Colonel Crawley did.'

'Did you on that occasion absolutely refuse to make any alteration in your detailed medical case as sent in by you the day before?'

This question was not one the doctor was ready to answer without explanation as it called into question, at the very least, his judgment in a situation which had cost a man his life.

'At that interview which I had with Colonel Crawley I said that I did not consider that any additional report from me was necessary as I was convinced that he died from heat apoplexy, and that I had no proof that excess of spirits was the cause of his death and, to the best of my recollection, two hours afterwards I sent in my additional report, the addenda.

'I wish to add that when Assistant Surgeon Barnett reported to me in the morning that he had received information from Colonel Crawley with regard to the spirituous liquor which had been consumed by the sergeant-major, Assistant Surgeon Barnett informed me that he had asked Colonel Crawley that morning . . .'

Without doubt, Dr Turnbull was going on to say that Colonel Crawley had told Dr Barnett that he did not want a further report regarding the liquor* and that he was dealing with that aspect of the case himself.

But the president intervened: 'This is no answer to the question.'

Sensing that the tide of cross-examination was running for him at this moment, Colonel Crawley rapped out:

'Did you or did you not refuse to make any additional report in consequence of that interview?'

'At that time I did.'

'Do you or do you not mean to state that when a man dies of heat apoplexy the question whether he was or was not in the habit of consuming a large quantity of spirits daily is *not* a proper element to be considered and enquired into as part of such a detailed medical case?'

'Yes, I do consider that it should be enquired into.'

Having gained this point Colonel Crawley turned to other matters that might suggest that Dr Turnbull was not everything a regimental doctor should be. Anything, of course, that suggested that Turnbull had sought to conceal relevant facts or had allowed personal feelings to outweigh his professional judgment could only benefit Colonel Crawley's side of the case.

The colonel produced the hospital case-book from Mhow.

* See page 133.

It appeared that Dr Turnbull had, at the request of the divisional commander, sent in a certified extract from the case-book showing that Sergeant-Major Wakefield had been detained in hospital under observation, being 'feverish and excited' on hearing of Lilley's death.

But this entry, relating to 25 May, the day of Lilley's death, was not entered in the hospital book until 5 June—and after other entries had been made. On the face of it, it was a curious departure from what might be regarded as the normal routine of hospital records.

Colonel Crawley asked: 'You have said that Sergeant-Major Wakefield was admitted into hospital on 25 May for three days, and he then left hospital. Was there no entry made at the time of that admission and discharge in any book you can produce, and if not, why not?'

'He was merely detained in hospital,' said Dr Turnbull. 'His entry was not made in any case-book at the time on 25 May.'

'Did I not, on 27 June, call your attention to the statement* that Sergeant-Major Wakefield had been sent to hospital on 25 May as a raving maniac, and complain to you that you had not informed me that he had *not been in hospital at all at that date*: and did you not on that occasion tell me that you knew he had never been in hospital at that time, and could have told me so if I had asked you?'

The doctor's reply to this multiple question was brief, abrupt and again expressive of his resentment of the colonel:

'Yes, Colonel Crawley did. Yes. I do not remember Colonel Crawley having ever asked me any such question. No, I did not.'

'Do you know that Sergeant-Major Lilley during his last illness, and within a few hours, took nearly a tumblerful of brandy?' the colonel continued.

'I do not.'

'If that was so, in your opinion as a medical man would that, considering the indisposition under which he was labouring, and the temperament of the patient, have inevitably produced a fatal result?'

'Yes, I think it would have had an injurious effect. The fatal result I cannot state.'

* In the local press.

The colonel now concluded his cross-examination with a question further designed to throw doubt and suggest collusion by the doctor with the man out of whose misfortunes and prejudice these proceedings had, at last, sprung.

'When did you last see or receive any communication from Mr Smales?'

Defiantly perhaps, Dr Turnbull replied: 'I saw Captain Smales in London a week yesterday. I received a private communication from Captain Smales last week; what date I do not recollect.'

One last question in re-examination by the prosecutor displayed once again Turnbull's willingness, anxiety almost, to bring down Crawley if he could.

'Do you wish,' he was asked, 'to qualify in any way the statement you have made to the court—that Colonel Crawley said to you when you applied for leave for Sergeant-Major Lilley to sit in the verandah, "Why, the sergeant-majors have morning and evening exercise, what more do they require?" '

'The only way I wish to qualify it is this—that Colonel Crawley replied in a harsh tone of voice to me, as if he was annoyed at my having made the remark. It struck me that Colonel Crawley felt annoyed at my asking for that additional indulgence.'

17

The old soldier's story

THE prosecution called a number of sentries and guard commanders, largely for the benefit of Colonel Crawley who was at liberty to question these men even if the prosecutor did not wish to ask them anything himself.

They all testified that they could not see through the chick that screened Mrs Lilley from sight, and that they never saw her in her night attire, nor received any complaint from either Mrs Lilley or her husband.

Private Francis Drabble told the colonel that he saw Lilley drink 'several glasses of brandy' during one of his periods of duty as a sentry. The R.S.M. had drunk from a tumbler. When Drabble had refused a drink offered to him, Lilley drank it himself.

Private Francis Johnson had been John Lilley's batman for three years until he was arrested.

Colonel Crawley asked: 'Was Sergeant-Major Lilley regular in the habit of drinking a certain amount of spirits the first thing in the morning?'

'He used to drink a certain amount, but not to excess. He used to take half a dram of arrack in a cup of coffee the first thing in the morning.'

'In your opinion, after his arrival in India was he a strong man in point of health, or was he frequently ill?'

'He was ill three times while he was in India before his arrest.'

'Was he a man that could drink a considerable quantity of spirits without showing its effects?'

'I could not say.'

Private John Atkin, a soldier with twenty years' service in the regiment, said that he had known Lilley from the time he first joined the Inniskillings. The sergeant-major had been respected and he was a hard-working man.

'Was Mrs Lilley unwell at any time that you were on sentry?'

Yes, Atkin recalled an occasion when Mrs Lilley had been dusting ornaments in the large room. The sergeant-major had told her she ought not to be working as it was bad for her. A few minutes later Mrs Lilley fell, fainting on to the sofa.

'The sergeant-major then went and got her some soda water,' said Atkin. 'She drank a little of it and threw it up. He then gave her some brandy. He gave her that three times. She threw that up twice, and the last time it remained on her stomach.'

'Did Mrs Lilley know of your being on sentry and did she do anything in consequence?'

'I don't know whether she knew I was on sentry then: she did once before, for she asked the sergeant-major who it was that was on sentry. He told her it was Atkin and she said she did not care about him: she would come outside, as he was a married man.'

This pathetic picture of the dying woman being tended by her husband, and her reluctance to be in the presence of any sentry except someone like Atkin, the old soldier whom she knew well, is perhaps evidence enough of the Lilleys' sufferings.

Sergeant George Bennett, the paymaster sergeant at Mhow, was also called so that he could be questioned by Crawley. The colonel's aim was to attempt to justify the need, as he saw it, to keep Lilley under constant surveillance.

Bennett said that he had been given money by Captain Smales to pass on to Troop Sergeant-Major Wakefield through a Sergeant Bernard whose quarters were next door to those of Wakefield.

It appeared that there was a hole in the dividing wall between the two bungalows and this was used to pass messages through.

'Were any messages or questions to your knowledge conveyed to Sergeant-Major Lilley during his arrest?' asked Crawley.

'Paymaster Smales told me that he had corresponded nearly every day with Sergeant-Major Lilley during the time he was under arrest,' replied Sergeant Bennett.

What was not referred to at this stage, but must have been in the minds of some of those present, was that however clandestinely Smales may have been in communication with Lilley, he had a perfect right to do so in preparing and conducting his defence; and the colonel's preventing him from conferring with his witness was but one shameful aspect of the unfair trial of Captain Smales at Mhow.

Lieutenant-Colonel Fitzwygram, who had been second-in-command of the 6th Inniskilling Dragoons, had known Lilley for about twenty years and was called to give evidence as to his character.

He described him as 'one of the best men I ever met. With regard to his sobriety . . . I believe that my intercourse with him from the time he became my sergeant-major up to the time I left the regiment in 1860 was so constant and so continuous that it is impossible that he could have been addicted to drink without my having some knowledge or, at least, suspicion of it.'

Colonel Crawley produced a slightly different impression of Lilley from Troop Sergeant-Major George Henry Garroway, who had occupied the second bungalow before it was taken over to house Mr and Mrs Lilley.

'What is your opinion of these quarters in respect of their accommodation and comfort?'

'They were as good as any other sergeant-major's quarters in the regiment.'

'Were they hotter or cooler than the troop rooms occupied by the soldiers?' asked Crawley.

'I consider them cooler. They had a canvas roof underneath the tiles that prevented the heat penetrating into the room.'

Garroway said that he knew Lilley well and was on very good terms with him.

'Can you state whether or not he was in the habit of consuming a certain quantity of stimulants?'

Yes, Garroway knew Lilley to drink regularly. He drank brandy.

'I have known him one morning in particular to drink seven or eight glasses of brandy and soda water. . . . In the course of conversation with him he has told me he always drank arrack and coffee in the morning.'

What sort of man Mr Garroway was, or how he gave his evidence, or what impression it may have given, is not known. He left the courtroom but was almost immediately called back to answer a question by the prosecutor. If Mr Garroway had given any sort of impression that Lilley was a drunkard, Colonel Horsford's one short enquiry may have dispelled it.

'Did you respect Sergeant-Major Lilley?'

'I did.'

The prosecution's final piece of evidence was a letter written by the Inspector-General of Hospitals at Army Headquarters, Simla, India, on 20 July 1863.

It contained the inspector-general's opinion on Colonel Crawley's report of the amount of drink delivered to Lilley's quarters.

The inspector-general wrote:

'The fact that the quantities of spirits, wine and beer were sent to Sergeant-Major Lilley's quarters seems to be clearly established; but for the inference that he must have drunk the whole no proof has been adduced. On the contrary, his dying wife seems to have been recommended to take from three to four glasses of brandy daily, in small quantities, during the twenty-four hours.

'But the remainder, over and above the quantities ordered for Mrs Lilley, if consumed steadily by any ordinary individual, should have kept such individual in a state of almost chronic drunkenness.

'Sergeant-Major Lilley however, from several testimonies adduced, seems to have possessed great powers of resistance to the ordinary physical effects of drink. . . . If therefore the late sergeant-major could take eight glasses of brandy and soda water of a morning (without being unfit for duty) he may have taken a not greater quantity in the course of a day without showing any marked effects of drink.'

The medical report continued: 'But although the ordinary indications of being under the influence of drink may not have been noticeable, no man—especially one of Sergeant-Major

Lilley's large corpulent habit of body—could take spirits to the extent of six or seven glasses of brandy daily while confined in even the best N.C.O.'s quarter in the hot season in a climate like that at Mhow—and deprived moreover of his usual active bodily exercise, and no doubt depressed in mind by the unfortunate circumstances in which he had placed himself—without an almost certainty of a fatal attack of apoplexy. . . .

'It is impossible, without disbelieving the evidence submitted, to believe otherwise than that Sergeant-Major Lilley had been generally an intemperate man, and that he drank freely during his arrest; and that these habits of intemperance, under the painful circumstances in which he was placed, were the strong predisposing, if not the immediate exciting cause of his fatal attack, whether that attack be called heat apoplexy, or apoplexy induced by intemperance; for both causes, the heat and the climate and intemperance in ardent spirits always react on and aggravate each other. (Signed) G. S. Beatson, M.D.'

This opinion that Lilley had virtually brought his death upon himself by his drinking was, of course, really evidence for the defence, but, being an official document, it was produced by the prosecution.

Whether such an equitable procedure would have been followed at Mhow, had such evidence existed in the case of Captain Smales, may be doubted.

18

The Indian's story

THE main burden of Colonel Crawley's defence had rested so far on cross-examination of prosecution witnesses. His own witnesses were few, and so the presentation of the defence case was brief. The colonel continued to rely upon evidence to suggest that the prosecution witnesses were, to say the least, unreliable; and that Sergeant-Major Lilley had been a heavy drinker.

His first witness was Captain Francis George Savage Curtis, an officer who had been a colonel's man in the mess dispute that, by now, must have seemed so remote and tiresome to all concerned.

'Were you present at the Mhow court martial when Sergeant-Major Lilley was examined and made the statement as to the indignity suffered by his wife?' asked Crawley.

'I was. I was sitting quite close to Colonel Crawley. . . . I can remember Colonel Crawley's look of astonishment, and he turned to me and said, "Good God, can this be true?" '

Captain Curtis also recalled witnessing the demonstration of affection by the regiment when Colonel Crawley left to face trial in England.

Two members of the court at Mhow also testified to Crawley's apparent surprise when Lilley referred to the closeness of the sentries to his wife's bed. They were Captain William Henry James Clarke of the 72nd Highlanders and Captain John MacNeil of the same regiment. The prosecutor did not cross examine either of them.

A more controversial witness for the defence was Ardaseer Framjee, the Parsee merchant who kept the camp liquor store. He formally produced an account of Sergeant-Major Lilley's purchases during April and May, covering the now notorious quantity of brandy, port and gin.

'Did Sergeant-Major Lilley frequently come to your shop before his arrest?' asked Colonel Crawley.

'He did.'

'Was he in the habit of drinking anything at your shop?'

'He did. Two or three glasses of brandy and soda water.'

'Did you supply him with the brandy without payment?'

'Yes, I did.'

'Why did you do that?'

'He was my best customer.'

'How long were you in the habit of supplying him with liquor without payment?'

'Since the arrival of the regiment in India.'

Ardaseer Framjee produced an extract from his account covering one year's purchases of liquor by Lilley. The bill worked out at an average of nine bottles of brandy a month, not counting gin, port and ale.

The importance of this evidence to the defence was that, if accepted, it showed that Lilley was buying—if not consuming—large amounts of alcoholic drink *before* his wife's health reached the final stage when she was being kept alive virtually by brandy. It tended to establish Lilley as a steady drinker over a long period.

The prosecutor took over the questioning.

'To whom did you give that bill which has your signature?'

'Colonel Crawley . . . he said he wanted a copy of it for twelve months previous to the sergeant-major dying.'

Crawley intervened to say that he had been asked to get this bill by order of Sir Hugh Rose, the Commander-in-Chief, India.

Extracting the accounts required from Ardaseer Framjee had evidently been a lengthy undertaking, for the Indian said:

'I go to Colonel Crawley's bungalow every day. Many times I go. Many times I speak about the accounts.'

After further questions about the accounts the prosecutor pointed out that although the bills for drink had been produced together with Framjee's books, the drink had mostly been supplied to Lilley's servant by Framjee's assistant and neither was present to give evidence.

'Therefore,' said Colonel Horsford, 'as the evidence now stands there is no proof whatever that any of the brandy included in this account was ever ordered by Sergeant-Major Lilley or ever reached him at all.'

There was perhaps here an implication that the evidence might have been concocted by Ardaseer Framjee with the connivance of Crawley or his adjutant, and Crawley, after a whispered consultation with his lawyer, objected, saying that these remarks should be left until the prosecutor's closing speech.

The court agreed that this would be the best course. They also agreed to Colonel Crawley's request for a week's adjournment to allow him to prepare his final address.

The court met again on 17 December 1863, the twenty-first day of the trial. Colonel Crawley addressed the court at very great length. He spoke all day. Not everything he said was relevant to the charges, but he was, of course, fighting for his professional and social existence, and emotion was inevitable in his plea.

It has also to be noted that it was not really Colonel Crawley's speech at all; a great deal of it was the work of his counsel, Mr Harcourt, an expert in emotional appeals to juries.

The colonel began by pointing out that this was his first opportunity to reply to the 'calumnies of the vilest kind' that had been spread by his enemies and repeated by others. His enemies were those he had had to reprove—a clear reference to Captain Smales, Lieutenant Fitzsimon and Dr Turnbull.

He spoke scathingly of the press—'the self-constituted social hangmen, who execute their unlovely office without the formality of a trial or the sanction of a sentence'.

Colonel Crawley was no doubt expressing the soldier's reaction to unbridled press comment on a number of military scandals involving autocratic behaviour that had come to light during mid-Victorian times.

Crawley was one of several officers whose activities had been publicised, although his case, involving the harrowing end of Sergeant-Major Lilley, appeared to be the worst of its kind.

Nevertheless, there was a feeling in the country that commanding officers, particularly in the cavalry, were too much a law unto themselves.

The colonel's speech touched upon the delicate matter of responsibility for the sergeant-major's being in close arrest. Why had not his superior officers, Major-General Farrell, Sir William Mansfield and Sir Hugh Rose been charged?

Sir Hugh and Sir William, Crawley pointed out, knew well that the 'Dominions of the Queen in Hindustan' were held by military tenure, and the basis of that tenure was military discipline.

'They have seen one mutiny and they have quelled it,' he said. 'They know out of what beginnings that dire cataclysm burst forth. They know how the dykes of discipline were broken down and the flood of mutiny overwhelmed us unawares. It began by pampered insubordination of N.C.O.s, and it ended in those scenes of dread and horror which are commemorated on the stones which cover the wall of Cawnpore.* Men who have witnessed such a calamity are not likely to be careless of the symptoms which heralded another.'

Here perhaps was the real cause of the unthinking confinement of Sergeant-Major Lilley: the reflex action of commanders grown hyper-sensitive to the slightest suggestion of insubordination while the Indian Mutiny was within recent memory.

As Colonel Crawley put it:

'Those who have charge of a powder magazine do not look at the sparks with indifference. They know that in such cases an early severity is the truest mercy, and they punish the first signs of insubordination with strictness in order that they may not have finally to suppress mutiny with bloodshed.

'Close arrest may be a severe measure, but it is better than blowing your soldiers from the guns.'

This was a reference to the barbaric practice of executing mutineers by tying them across the mouths of field guns and firing through their bodies.

In a general reference to the trouble he had had with some

* Entire British population of Cawnpore, including women and children, was massacred by Nona Sahib during the Mutiny in 1857.

of his officers, but about which he had been unable to call evidence since his manner towards his subordinates—criticised though it had been in the press—was not the subject of any charge, Colonel Crawley said:

'You have seen some of my officers. You have seen, you have heard enough I think of the men who have so comported themselves in a court of justice, to judge of what must have been my situation on the parade and in the mess room.

'You will readily believe that when disaffection has become chronic among the officers, it is not long before the infection begins to spread among those immediately below them. . . . What lessons do you think the sergeants of the regiment were likely to learn from such instructors? . . .

'The body of the regiment, it is true, was still sound; the discipline of the troops intact. But the crisis had arrived, the danger was imminent. One more step and the flame might have been kindled in the ranks, and the famous regiment of the Inniskilling Dragoons would have broken out into open mutiny. . . . Sir, the question which lies at the root of this whole matter is the question of mutiny or no mutiny.'

As the colonel progresses with his speech he gives an impression of becoming more and more convinced that he had been dealing at Mhow, not with a few N.C.O.s who had read the proceedings of Captain Smales' trial a few days before they appeared in the local newspapers, but that he had acted just in time to prevent a general uprising throughout his regiment.

Of course, when a man is faced with an accusation of any kind which it is difficult to deny, it is natural for him to try and justify the offence to himself. This natural reaction may have influenced Colonel Crawley's closing address. In his mind's eye he may have seen furtive, murmuring groups of soldiers, sidelong glances from N.C.O.s and officers, a regiment that was become a cauldron of unrest and about to boil over. The more dangerous the situation he conceived, the less blameworthy his own actions became.

Colonel Crawley now came to the crux of his speech, his plea on the specific charges laid against him. What he had said so far, even if it had been accepted as true in every particular, was no answer to the charges. It was necessary for him to convince the court that he had not used 'undue severity' and had not caused 'great and grievous hardship'.

His orders had been, and the object of the arrest was, to prevent communication between Lilley and 'persons outside', yet it was clear that communication had taken place.

'How was it done? I did not, I would not, separate him from his sick wife. The servants were watched for letters and papers. I could not expose Mrs Lilley to such an indignity. She visited her friends, she went about the barracks: she was, as Sergeant-Major Cotton tells you, frequently at his wife's quarters. Mr Smales was able to boast to his clerk that in spite of the regimental orders, in spite of the sentries, in spite of the close arrest, he communicated with Sergeant-Major Lilley every day.

'Sir, I think it is just possible that on this occasion Mr Smales told the truth. But if it is conceivable he should have done so, then the offence with which I am justly chargeable is not that of excessive severity, but of inexcusable laxity in the execution of the orders I received. . . .'

The implication was clear: Mrs Lilley, free from searching and able to move about the camp, was her husband's messenger and link between him and Captain Smales. She probably was: but who shall blame her?

Colonel Crawley passed to the subject of the quarters in which the Lilleys lived. His argument amounted to this: that the first bungalow was entirely adequate to their needs; the second, admittedly, left something to be desired but was equal to and better than some quarters occupied by others of Lilley's rank, and was the best available then that would meet the conditions of his close arrest and prevent his communicating with others.

It had yet to be pointed out to him that his argument about preventing communication was completely fallacious.

19

The colonel's plea

HAVING answered, as he supposed, the question of hardship arising out of the quarters in which the Lilleys were confined, Colonel Crawley turned his attention to other hardships that the prosecution had referred to. It had been suggested that Lilley did not get enough exercise.

'You saw how Surgeon Turnbull flinched on that question,' he said. 'If the exercise was insufficient in amount, or improper in quality, when did he remonstrate? And if he never remonstrated, why not?'

The colonel referred to and read out some brief cross-examination of Dr Turnbull by the president:

President: You have stated that the exercise taken by R.S.M. Lilley was in a great measure nullified by the manner in which it was carried out. What do you mean?

Dr Turnbull: I mean that the R.S.M. in his position as such would feel degraded at being marched up and down by an escort on the parade ground.

President: Did you make any representation to the commanding officer on the subject?

Dr Turnbull: No, I did not.

President: Was it not your duty as medical officer in charge to have done so?

Dr Turnbull: I considered it was a point of discipline I had no business to interfere in.

Colonel Crawley's contemptuous manner in recalling the doctor's discomfiture at this stage may be imagined.

In fact, of course, the doctor would probably have found it difficult to make his point to Crawley on medical grounds. If he had been able to say that in his opinion Lilley was not getting enough exercise, or that it ought to be taken more frequently, or if he had been able to make any other straightforward medical recommendation within the understanding of a layman, then Colonel Crawley would have disregarded it only at his own risk.

But for the doctor to suggest that the sergeant-major might feel 'degraded' at the form of the exercise, and thereby nullify its beneficial effect, would have been to rely on a psychological factor at a time when the science of the mind was not generally known or understood.

The doctor might have *felt* that the exercise was nullified, and have understood the reason for it; but how to explain that or rely upon it in opposing the will of the colonel?

Evidence is not fact, it is fact recalled; and in the process of recollection it is wrung dry of much of the original emotion and physical circumstances that surrounded it. At the time of the Mhow court martial Dr Turnbull would have found it an impossible undertaking to have influenced Colonel Crawley with such a fanciful medical theory, even if the colonel had been in a frame of mind to allow some amelioration of the sergeant-major's arrest.

It is likely that this opinion of Turnbull's, offered for the first time some two years after the event, did sound lame in the calm, judicial atmosphere of an English court martial.

Then too, if Dr Turnbull had lacked the moral courage of his medical convictions in Mhow while Sergeant-Major Lilley was still alive, his manner may well have lacked assurance with Lilley long dead and with his own character as an officer under assault in cross-examination.

Perhaps the greatest emotion in England had been aroused by the sufferings of Mrs Lilley. The colonel now had to deal with this highly dangerous element in the case against him.

'Next to the "bomb-proof oven" I think the greatest prominence has been given to the indignities said to have been suffered by Mrs Lilley. "All the functions of nature were performed by the dying woman in the presence of strange men",' he quoted from the speech made in the House of Commons.

'There is something so unmanly and so cowardly in the infliction of wanton indignity upon a sick and defenceless woman that the bare suggestion of such an act fires the indignation of every generous heart,' he said.

He recalled the evidence of Private Patrick Gaffney, who had been on sentry twice during Lilley's confinement in the large first bungalow.

He quoted the prosecutor's first question:

' "Can you tell the court anything about liniment being rubbed on Mrs Lilley's chest?" '

And the soldier's reply:

' "Yes. The second time I mounted guard about 10 o'clock, and I was about half an hour on sentry and the sergeant-major came to me and asked me to do him a kindness; to go outside the bungalow while his wife undressed—out of the room. He wanted to rub some liniment into her breast. I did so. When his wife was dressed I came back to my post." '

Colonel Crawley seemed to see in the humanity of Private Gaffney some counterpoise to the inhumanity which formed the basis of the principal charge against him.

'Sir, do you suppose these fine fellows did not think the suggestion of indignity to Mrs Lilley an imputation on their own honour no less than mine? . . .

'Where is the sentry who was within two feet of Mrs Lilley's bed? Why have the prosecution not produced him? They could not find him because he never existed.'

It was true that no sentry had been found to testify to being posted at such a distance from Mrs Lilley's bed, but the onus of finding such a man was on the prosecution, which had been prepared in England, months away from India by the communications of the time.

Two feet? Three feet? Four feet? Was there very much difference? The sentry was at the door of the bedroom in the first bungalow when Lilley was with his wife. It was not disputed that the bed was a few feet from the chick behind which the sentry stood. Dr Barnett had spoken of his being clearly visible; of the need to speak in undertones, and of his opinion that the sentry was 'an annoyance' to Mrs Lilley.

But Colonel Crawley saw some credit reflected upon himself in the consideration of Private Gaffney for Mrs Lilley's modesty.

'It was enough that Sergeant-Major Lilley wished the sentry to withdraw, and he did withdraw accordingly, as he says, "outside the bungalow".

'What was the *meaning* of the complaint made by Sergeant-Major Lilley at the Mhow court martial? Sir, I think you will find that the evidence of Private Atkin, who was examined on 2 December, explains completely the whole affair.

'It appears that on some day previous to 7 May 1862 Sergeant-Major Lilley made some complaint to the sentry. Of what character that complaint was we do not exactly know. That complaint ought to have been, and would have been, reported, and the cause of complaint removed, but for the following circumstances to which I ask your special attention. These are the exact words of the witness's evidence.

' "*Question:* Did you report that complaint?

' "*Answer:* No sir.

' "*Question:* State why you did not?

' "*Answer:* He wished me not to. He said he was going to the court himself in a few days and he would complain. I asked him if I should do so to the sergeant of the guard, and he said No."

'Now, sir,' continued Colonel Crawley, 'was the sentry within two feet of his wife's bed, and did he—when he was offered the certain redress which the complaint, if reported, would have procured—deliberately intend to leave his wife for a "few days" exposed to such an indignity in order that he might the better parade the complaint in open court?

'Even if that complaint had been true, what should we think of the man who thus sacrificed his wife to his revenge?'

Colonel Crawley was conscious of the fact that, to the public, he was the man who had branded the dead sergeant-major a drunkard so as to absolve himself from responsibility for his death. He turned to this question of Lilley's character.

'The prosecution have sought to build up a case against me by accumulating irrelevant testimony to the excellence of Sergeant-Major Lilley's character. I shall leave them undisturbed in the possession of all the advantage they expect to derive from it. My only reply shall be this: if Sergeant-Major Lilley had been the most perfect of created beings; if he had been a model of all the non-commissioned officers that ever existed, and yet had on this occasion been guilty of a grave act of insubordination—and that the prosecution do not deny—it was my duty to punish him for it. And the better the man the worse the example, and therefore the more necessary the punishment. . . .

'But, sir, when it is sought, upon the testimony of the doctors, to fix me with a personal liability for the death of Sergeant-Major Lilley, it becomes necessary for me to demonstrate the whole truth of the case which they have so sedulously laboured to conceal. . . .

'The case for the prosecution on the medical part of the subject seems to be this: they say that the death of Sergeant-Major Lilley must have been due to the severity of his confinement because there was no other assignable reason for it.'

The colonel spoke bitterly of the evidence of Dr Barnett who, he claimed, had tried to minimise the amount of spirits that Lilley's wife had told him her husband drank.

'But, sir, this question of the brandy does not depend on the admission of Mrs Lilley alone, nor upon the unwilling testimony of Dr Barnett. . . . What does Lance-Corporal Holman tell you?

'On the night of 23 May, the night before the first symptoms of his illness appeared, Sergeant-Major Lilley takes a bottle of brandy from under the couch on the verandah—out of a long boot. A man does not keep his wife's medicine in a long boot under his own bed. . . .'

It was a good point, and would have had even more force if the issue had simply been whether or not Sergeant-Major Lilley had been an habitually heavy drinker. But, of course, it was not.

It would be tedious to go through the colonel's lengthy argument about the second charge concerning responsibility for the placing of the sentries. Briefly, he founded his case upon an assertion that the annoyance to Mrs Lilley had never occurred.

'The second charge involves a double untruth. It involves first the untruth that Mrs Lilley's privacy was intruded upon; and secondly, the untruth that it was intruded upon by my order.'

After a further review of the evidence the colonel wondered aloud how he could have known there was reason for complaint in Lilley's confinement.

'The adjutant did not tell me; the orderly officer did not tell me; the doctors did not tell me of any complaint. And why did they not tell me of any complaint, except for the best of all reasons?—that the man himself made no complaint because he had nothing to complain of.'

Listening to Colonel Crawley's closing speech to the court, his audience might understandably have asked themselves at this point: what, then, is this all about? Why are we here? The colonel, it seemed, was dismissing the whole case against himself as being groundless.

It was true that there had been no official complaint made by Lilley before his dramatic reference in court to the sentry. Whether no complaint had been made direct to Colonel Crawley for fear of bringing some further burden to existence upon the wretched couple is a question that the Lilleys took with them unanswered to their graves.

If such things as had been suggested had really happened would not the whole regiment have 'been in arms against the tyrant?' the colonel asked.

He reminded the court of the scene when he had left Mhow.

'What a spectacle! The murderer of Sergeant-Major Lilley is pursued by the cheers and blessings of the brothers-in-arms of the injured man. They bid him God-speed in the hour of his trial. They pray for the return of this harsh, wicked, unjust, tyrannical colonel.'

As is customary at courts martial, the sword of the accused man lay on the table before the court. In due time, when the court had reached a verdict it would be placed point towards the colonel if they had found him guilty, or hilt towards him if he were not guilty.

Perhaps Colonel Crawley's eye caught the sword as he came to the end of his speech and prompted his closing words; or perhaps, like the rest of the speech, it had been carefully prepared and written out in collaboration with his counsel.

'You will give me back my character,' said Colonel Crawley, 'you will give me back my sword; a sword which has been for thirty years—aye, and which shall be again—at the service of a nation at whose hands, in the language of the charge, I have suffered "great and grievous hardships".'

The colonel then called twenty-four witnesses to speak of the excellence of his character, both as an officer and as a man.

The defence was over. Some of Colonel Crawley's phrases perhaps fall awkwardly upon the ear today; but emotion was fashionable a century ago.

It was but two years since the Queen herself had embarked upon a public display of grief in widowhood that was to last another thirty-seven years.

If a colonel of dragoons, fighting against the prospect of professional and social ruin, employed over-dramatic tones and cadences to reinforce his final verbal effort before surrendering himself to judgment, it was in keeping with the man's time, and with the man himself.

20

The prosecutor's reply

DRAMA and emotion are inherent in a defence at law. The ingredients of the case may increase the drama or intensify the emotion, but the basic drama of the defence is always there—because there is something at stake for the prisoner: at worst it may be his life.

In the literal sense Colonel Crawley's life was not at stake, but in another sense it was. If he were to be found guilty he would be branded as unfit to command a regiment: he was, in any case, 'only upon trial' as officer commanding the 6th Inniskilling Dragoons since publication of the Duke of Cambridge's memorandum following Lilley's death.

A verdict of guilty meant the virtual end of Crawley's career in the army, however lenient a sentence might be passed upon him. Resignation of his commission or early retirement were inevitable consequences, even if he were not cashiered.

There were the almost equally important social consequences. A verdict of guilty would endorse every calumny written or spoken about him; his notoriety would be perpetuated.

A prosecutor, on the other hand, has nothing at stake—except perhaps personal vanity or satisfaction—and can therefore present his case in a more detached manner.

Colonel Sir Alfred Horsford was detached and cool, and professional: he had had the assistance of the deputy Judge Advocate, Mr Denison. He agreed with Colonel Crawley that some of the things that had been said about him in the press and other places were not true, but he qualified his agreement with some deliberation:

'Such mis-statements and exaggerations are extremely to be regretted, not only for the sake of the prisoner—to whom they are most unfair—but also because they render the administration of justice difficult by raising prejudices and causing misapprehensions which, when corrected by a knowledge of the actual facts, make those facts seem less important and serious than they really are.'

Colonel Horsford's meaning was clear: if Colonel Crawley was not as black as he had been painted in the newspapers, he might, nevertheless, be a rather dark shade of grey.

The colonel began a quiet review of the case for the prosecution. He pointed out that there was no question about the legality of the order to keep the three sergeants in close arrest so far as Crawley was concerned. What the court were concerned about was the way in which it had been done.

The alleged conspiracy with which the sergeant-majors were charged had been directed against Crawley; the trial of Smales was on at the time—in which Crawley was both prosecutor and defendant; Lilley was a witness against the colonel in that trial; the Commander-in-Chief had ruled there was insufficient evidence to support a charge of conspiracy; it was within the colonel's discretion to have allowed Lilley to communicate with anyone during his close arrest; Captain Smales 'was entitled by law as freely to communicate with the sergeant-major as Colonel Crawley has been allowed to communicate, not only with his witnesses, but even with the witnesses for the prosecution' in the present trial.

In all these circumstances, Colonel Horsford suggested that a commanding officer who had to keep a sergeant-major in close arrest would naturally feel himself placed in as delicate and responsible a position as could well be imagined: a position where 'on the one hand, all the noble qualities which go to make up the character of an officer might be nobly illustrated; where, on the other hand, all the undefined and discretionary powers which are necessarily entrusted to a commanding officer might be terribly abused'.

He pointed out that in this case these discretionary powers could be used for three purposes, perhaps: 'first, to gratify feelings of anger and dislike towards an individual; secondly, to obstruct the defence of another individual against whom Crawley was then acting as prosecutor, and for whom the first-named individual was a witness; thirdly, to facilitate his own justification in his character of defendant before the Mhow court martial.'

Sir Alfred said he would show, from the evidence on record, that Colonel Crawley actually did employ the discretionary powers which he had as commanding officer 'precisely in this manner and for these purposes'.

'Let us now follow the arrest through its several stages of severity. The course of the arrest, as proved by the evidence, was this: at its commencement on 26 April 1862 it was simple arrest. Later in the same day it was close arrest, under a sentry placed outside the quarters. Shortly afterwards it was close arrest under a sentry placed inside the quarters.

'Shortly afterwards it was close arrest under a sentry placed in the very same rooms with the sergeant-majors with positive orders not to lose sight of the prisoners day or night.

'This gradually increasing scale of severity was ordered by whom? And under what pretext?'

Colonel Horsford referred to a letter which Crawley had written on 4 June 1862 to Major-General Farrell, the Mhow divisional commander, when enquiries were first being made into Lilley's death.

He had written: 'In consequence of the impossibility of preventing communication being held with the prisoners by parties in the interest of Paymaster Smales, it was deemed advisable to place the sentries in the rooms with the prisoners, not only to avoid the exposure of the sentries to the sun and hot winds, but to prevent the witnesses being tampered with during the remainder of the trial.'

Another letter, which Crawley had thought to be to his advantage, was also cited by Colonel Horsford as evidence against him.

When Crawley wrote to Major-General Farrell on 24 May, Lilley's last full day of life, suggesting that the close arrest might be eased, he had written:

'Now that Paymaster Smales has made his defence there is no longer a necessity for keeping the three sergeant-majors in close arrest with sentries over them lest they should be tampered with.'

Thus, said the prosecutor, it was clear that the real object of the close arrest and of placing the sentries inside the rooms was solely concerned with the defence of Paymaster Smales whose witnesses they were.

Colonel Horsford went on to point out that Smales closed the case for his defence on 10 May 1862, and so the only reason for keeping sentries in the three men's rooms—to prevent their being tampered with as witnesses—had ceased to exist from that date: they had, by then, given their evidence.

'I need hardly observe to this court that this prohibition of all communication, verbal or written, between Mr Smales and his witnesses (by whomsoever it was ordered) was absolutely illegal; nor need I contrast with that proceeding in India the proceeding of the Crown here with regard to the free access which Colonel Crawley has been permitted to have, not only to his own witnesses but also to those for the prosecution, both in India and in England.'

The prosecutor reminded the court that Captain Smales had been given seven days in which to prepare his closing defence speech at Mhow and that because he was unwell the court had been further adjourned until 24 May.

'Therefore, from 10 May to 25 May, which was the day of Sergeant-Major Lilley's death—that is for a space of fifteen days—it is proved beyond all possibility of question by the prisoner's own showing in his own written official statements, and by the record of the proceedings of the Mhow court martial, that the sentry was kept inside Sergeant-Major Lilley's quarters absolutely without any reason whatever, and kept there by the mere arbitrary exercise of the discretionary power entrusted to the prisoner as commanding officer.'

As to the 'great and grievous hardship' caused to the Lilleys, Colonel Horsford made the contemptuous comment:

'The court will have observed that throughout the examination of the witnesses Colonel Crawley has seemed to think—and to suppose that this court would think—that the opinions of the sentries about the annoyance and inconvenience endured by Mrs Lilley furnished the true test of the reality and amount of that annoyance and inconvenience, and that the proper mode of arriving at a knowledge of her feelings would be to ask some of the sentries what *their* feelings on the matter were.

'What will this court think of such a test of a woman's feelings?

'It seems strange indeed to suppose that this court would think such a thing as a chick could be an obstacle to the vexation with which the known presence of a sentry must have struck the dying woman; a vexation that did not depend on the mere fact of the sentry seeing or hearing her, but on the fixed, ever-present knowledge in her mind that there was about her bed and about her path, and spying out all her ways, a constantly shifting, watchful, male stranger, who seemed to be by law not only entitled always to be there, but whose duty it was to be so.

'Surely so flimsy an argument is as easily seen through as the chick itself?'

As to Lilley's supposed heavy drinking, Colonel Horsford asked: 'Does it aid the defence to show that a singularly superior soldier was driven by misery to drink?'

He recalled the evidence of Cornet Snell concerning the day of Lilley's complaint. Crawley had asked Snell if it was true that a sentry stood within two feet of Mrs Lilley's bed; and when told that it was so, asked who gave the order.

Colonel Horsford read the transcript of Cornet Snell's evidence:

' "Colonel Crawley then said: *I ordered close arrest; why are my orders not properly carried out? Do you know what close arrest is, Mr Snell?*

' "I answered that I thought I did.

' "Colonel Crawley said: *Go and see that my orders are properly carried out.*

' "I then left the mess. That was all, sir, and that is as nearly the tenour of the conversation as I can possibly remember.

' "I then went to the sergeant-major's bungalow and changed the position of the sentry, placing him in the lobby or small room next the dining room. I placed him there with the order that he was in no way to interfere with Mrs Lilley but not to lose sight of Sergeant-Major Lilley except when he went into his wife's bedroom." '

From the rest of Cornet Snell's evidence it appeared that

later in the day he handed Colonel Crawley a copy of the orders he had given the sentry. The colonel, without reading them, handed them back to him, saying: 'Do you think, Mr Snell, I am a lance-corporal to write out orders for a guard?'

Colonel Horsford dropped the transcript of evidence on the table before him.

'This evidence of Cornet Snell, whose youth, manner and demeanour carried with them evidence of absolute sincerity, seems to prove plainly enough first, that in order to obviate the evils consequent on Colonel Crawley's former order, some change in the terms of that order was absolutely necessary.

'Secondly, that such change was made by Mr Snell after being informed by the colonel, though only impliedly, that some change was necessary.

'Thirdly, that Colonel Crawley was actually informed by Cornet Snell that he had framed a new order and that he showed the colonel this new order.

'Fourthly, that the colonel took no steps himself to ascertain whether such new order was a proper one, but threw the whole responsibility of taking care that Mrs Lilley was not annoyed further on this very young officer—an officer who had never done the duty of adjutant before—and this on the very same day on which, according to Colonel Crawley's statement, no person could be more shocked than he had been to learn that Mrs Lilley had been annoyed by the former order.'

Colonel Horsford said that Crawley's way of dealing with his subordinates throughout Lilley's arrest threw all responsibility off himself and upon them.

'Let us now, lastly, apply to this matter the simplest of tests —that of equal justice.

'The colonel was ordered to keep the three sergeant-majors in arrest and not to release them till Mr Smales' trial was over. That order came from Sir William Mansfield and, though it has been pronounced illegal, the colonel has not been deemed responsible for having obeyed it because it was not clearly illegal on its face and its terms were precise and explicit. Therefore, the responsibility of ordering the arrest rests with the authority who gave the order.

'Why is not the same measure that has been meted out to Colonel Crawley to be meted out to his adjutant? For the cases are precisely similar. Colonel Crawley's orders were not clearly illegal on the face, and therefore, the adjutant was bound to obey them. He did so to the letter. Why then is he to be held responsible? And why is the responsibility not to rest with the authority who gave the order? If a general officer is responsible for an order given by him to the colonel of a regiment, why is not a colonel of a regiment to be responsible for an order given by him to his adjutant? Yet it is this plain rule of right which you are asked to adjudge to be wrong, and to give to that judgment the sanction of your several names in the weight of your collective authority.'

Colonel Sir Alfred Horsford was simply doing his duty as prosecutor, but some of his phrases seem to suggest that he did not personally have much regard for Colonel Crawley. The contempt implicit in some of his remarks perhaps went beyond the contrived emotion of an advocate.

'The court will not have failed to observe,' he went on, 'that whenever the testimony of a witness is adverse to the prisoner it is regarded by the defence as perjury.'

He referred, like Colonel Crawley, to the evidence of Private Atkin, to whom Lilley first complained about the position of the sentry.

Colonel Crawley's observation—that if the complaint had been true and Lilley had waited until he could raise it in open court, such prolongation of his wife's embarrassment was despicable—may well have been valid.

But if the position of the sentry had not been as Lilley described it, Colonel Horsford wondered whether Private Atkin was to be considered a perjurer also?

The prosecutor made it quite clear that in his opinion Lilley had been telling the truth when he complained, whatever might be thought of his delay in making the complaint.

Concluding his speech, Colonel Horsford said:

'Colonel Crawley has stated that Sir William Mansfield's letter of 6 May reached Mhow on 12 May. Therefore he must have known on that day of Sir William Mansfield's authoritative declaration that the sergeant-majors could not be arraigned on a charge of conspiracy, and that there was no sufficient evidence of their having committed that crime. And yet Colonel Crawley has actually called upon the court to believe that he was warranted in treating them with as much severity as a court of ordinary criminal jurisdiction would treat a convicted offender.

'Colonel Crawley says: "This case has been treated as one of peculiar military barbarity. But I must be permitted to ask in what respect the execution of military law differs in this respect from that of civil sentences."

'Thus Colonel Crawley really claims the right to regard the three sergeant-majors as having been *actually undergoing sentence*, even after Sir William Mansfield had declared that they could not even be tried for the offence which they were alleged to have committed, and that there was not sufficient evidence of their having committed any offence at all.

'Does not this furnish some clue to the undue and unnecessary and utterly illegal severity of the prisoner towards these men?'

There was an outburst of clapping and murmurs of approval from the 'lower end' of the court where the non-commissioned ranks were crowded behind the barrier.

The prosecutor had finished, and it was now the turn of the Judge Advocate General, who stands rather in the position of a civil judge at a court martial, to sum up. The court itself—the senior officers sitting in judgment upon Colonel Crawley—were more like a jury, except that they would not only decide whether or not he was guilty, but would, in private discussion among themselves, arrive at an agreed sentence if that should be required.

The Judge Advocate's remarks do not form part of the court record, but, just as an ordinary judge would do, he no doubt told the court that if in anything he said he appeared to be expressing an opinion of his own then they would disregard that and judge the matter solely upon the facts. This, it must be assumed, they did.

It is not clear from the record how long it took the court to arrive at its verdict, but it appears not to have been a lengthy retirement for the proceedings officially ended at a quarter tc four in the afternoon. The prosecutor's speech would have taken the whole morning, so the court probably took about an hour to find Colonel Crawley not guilty on both charges.

The colonel's sword was returned to him with due formality, and the court recorded that it 'cannot close its proceedings without remarking on the animus displayed by Major Swindley when giving his evidence, and on the evasive, hesitating, unsatisfactory character of the evidence of Surgeon Turnbull and Lieutenant and Adjutant Fitzsimon and on the manner in which their evidence was given'.

The verdict, reached on Friday, 18 December 1863, was approved by the Queen on 23 December and published on that day.

21

After the trial

THE Queen's approval was very far from being echoed throughout the land. All the daily newspapers with the exception of *The Times* and *Morning Advertiser* found fault with the verdict. Members of the public continued to write to editors defending or attacking the notorious colonel.

The Times, which had long been a forum for debating the Crawley case, had changed its ground more than once during the trial.

At one stage, before the evidence was concluded, the paper appeared to favour an acquittal; but on 21 December with, as it were, Sir Alfred Horsford's concluding speech still very much in mind, the leader-writer was adopting a somewhat judicial attitude, but one from which a leap in either direction, depending on the verdict, was possible.

Thus *The Times*: 'It is right that all this unhappy couple went through should be known, since it has been called into question, but it would be very wrong that we should confound their misfortunes with their wrongs. We have not to consider so much what they felt as what the colonel did, and with what motive.

'The story cannot be otherwise than sad, but it is a suspicion of tyranny which gives the sting to the trouble and makes intolerable that which, if regarded as a dispensation of Providence, or even as a legal penalty, would be only lamentable.

'This tyrannical intent is, and has been from the first, the gist of the allegations against Colonel Crawley. Whether he be convicted or acquitted by the court martial, it is by his motives, as evidenced by his language and acts throughout this affair, that he must stand or fall at the bar of public opinion.'

This was three days before the verdict was published. Since

the colonel's language and most of his acts in evidence pointed to his vindictiveness towards Lilley, this last observation of *The Times* seems to find him morally guilty in advance whatever the verdict.

Came 23 December and the Queen's approval of the acquittal.

On 24 December *The Times* said: 'It is not too much to say that not only the charges formally made by the prosecution, but every imputation upon him that was tested by legal evidence in the course of the enquiry, signally broke down. . . . Lilley's wife, being ill, might have been admitted to the female hospital, but naturally preferred to stay with her husband. . . .

'There is really no reason to suppose that she experienced any inconvenience or "indignity" whatever. We would not utter a harsh or unfeeling word of Mrs Lilley for whose character Colonel Crawley himself expresses a high respect; but truth is truth, and we cannot help saying that a great deal of false delicacy has been wasted, in our opinion, upon this part of the subject.

'Privacy is a relative term: a sergeant's wife is not accustomed to the same sort of privacy as a fine lady, and to say that Mrs Lilley's modesty was wantonly insulted because a sentry might possibly have seen her lying in bed if he chose to look through the lining of a chick or the folds of a curtain appears to us absurd. . . .

'We consider it to be clearly established that Colonel Crawley had no intention to persecute Lilley, but that no persecution was practised is the sufficient answer to the whole charge. . . .

'Everything points to the conclusion that he was more sinned against than sinning and succeeded to a command which would have tried the sagacity of a statesman and the patience of a saint.'

With this piece of stupefying snobbery *The Times* came round safe on course with the Establishment again.

The newspaper also refused to publish a lengthy letter from Mr D. Fortescue, the member of parliament who had first drawn the attention of the general public to the fate of John and Clarissa Lilley, and who felt that some further statement was due from him in view of the verdict and some apparent inaccuracies in his original speech in the Commons.

The *Daily News* took a different view of the verdict and was perhaps representative of the anti-Crawley press opinion:

'We are at a loss to understand how anyone who has read attentively the admirable reply of Sir Alfred Horsford can doubt that if Colonel Crawley had been tried by an ordinary jury he must have been convicted; can doubt that he was guilty of unjustifiable severity towards Lilley, and that he, not the adjutant, was responsible for the manner in which the close arrest was executed. . . .

'It is conclusively established that on the 3rd or 4th May Colonel Crawley gave a positive, peremptory, and precise order that the sentries were to be placed as not to lose sight of Sergeant-Major Lilley by night or by day.

'This order was given to the adjutant in the presence and hearing of six other witnesses, and the colonel insisted that it should be literally enforced notwithstanding the remonstrance of those present who declared that if enforced it would annoy and inconvenience Mrs Lilley. Will anyone pretend to believe that if Colonel Crawley, who gave the order, had been a corporal, and Lilley, who suffered, had been a private, the fifteen generals and colonels at Aldershot would have hesitated for one moment to hold the corporal who gave that order responsible for all consequences? . . .

'No sergeant-major has ever been treated so before and Sergeant-Major Lilley had enjoyed a spotless character until the fatal moment when Colonel Crawley took the command. But men must stick by their order. Public opinion must not be allowed to interfere with the discipline of the army.

'The rank and file are of different race from the "officers and gentlemen". The wives of soldiers—even of non-commissioned officers—are not fine ladies. There is a great gulf fixed between the two classes which it would be revolutionary to fill up. To place a sentry within a few yards of a fine lady's bed would be, of course, intolerable, but to place a sentry over Mrs Lilley's bed, we are told, was neither indecent nor even indelicate. . . .

'It is admitted that a great wrong has been done by someone, and that wrong must be redressed. It is a maxim of law that the King can do no wrong, and it seems to be a maxim of the army that a military officer can do no wrong. It was so in the Crimea. It is so still. This hocus-pocus may serve its turn sometimes: but now that it is admitted that the liberty of the subject has been trampled underfoot, and that the rights of the three sergeant-majors have been violated, it is absolutely essential that public justice should be vindicated.'

A Mr James Aytoun, writing from the Reform Club on 28 December, informed readers of the *Morning Advertiser*:

'. . . Colonel Crawley is not tried for the real offence—that is the illegal prolongation of the arrest. The Horse Guards order the issue to be confined to the manner in which the close arrest is carried out. . . . The whole question which the public wished to see investigated is shirked, given the go-by . . .

'Let us suppose a case occurring of a murder and that the man charged were accused of picking the pocket of the deceased after murdering him. What would we think of the magistrate who ordered the trial to be confined to the pocket-picking, while the murder was passed over altogether? . . .

'The Duke of Cambridge said some years ago that the battles of the Alma, Inkerman and our other successes in the Crimea were soldiers' victories—meaning that they were gained by the superior fighting qualities of our common soldiers and not by the skill of the officers.

'The public is quite aware of this truth, and regards the question now before us as one in which the rights and privileges of the privates of the army are involved. The people of England will not allow the soldiers who fight our battles and pour out their blood for the nation to be tyrannised over, oppressed, degraded and insulted—they and their wives—by the mere popinjays of the parade.'

Mr Fortescue, denied the platform of *The Times* from which to make a further statement, took the first opportunity available to him to raise the Lilley-Crawley affair again in the House of Commons.

This opportunity came on 15 March 1864. Mr Fortescue said he did not wish to call into question the verdict at Aldershot. There had been a conflict of evidence and, in accordance with the just and well recognised principles of British law, the construction most favourable to the accused had been accepted. Whatever his own opinion might be, he said he did not intend to disclose it.

Commenting on the different types of bungalows in which the Lilleys had lived during the arrest, the details of which had been unknown to him when he had first raised the subject of the Mhow court martial, Mr Fortescue said: 'I desire to express my regret that, either from a defect in the information supplied to me, or from an unconscious exaggeration of it on my part, I was led, in however small a degree, to overstate the facts of the case, and to add a shade, darker than the strict truth warranted, to a picture which required no assistance.'

Mr Fortescue spoke at some length about the legality of the arrest of the sergeant-majors, and said it appeared that the sanction and approval of his superiors absolved Colonel Crawley in the matter, while the verdict of the court martial acquitted him of all undue severity in its enforcement.

'The result is,' he said, 'that for all that occurred no one is responsible, and no one is to blame.'

There were murmurs of approval as he went on to say that that view of the matter had caused a great deal of dissatisfaction in the country.

It had confirmed the general distrust in courts martial and the administration of military justice. It had strengthened the general impression that in any issue between an inferior and his superior, every principle of justice, every consideration of fair play, was postponed and rendered subordinate to the one paramount object of what was called enforcing authority. How false and unfounded such means of enforcing authority were he need hardly discuss.

Replying for the government, the Marquess of Hartington said that when Mr Fortescue had first referred to the Mhow affair in the House the War Department had not been in a position to answer the various matters satisfactorily. It had been impossible to deny then, 'and is now equally impossible to deny . . . that in the opinion of the government Sergeant-Major Lilley died while he was confined in an illegal imprisonment, and that his death under such circumstances was a lamentable occurrence, calculated to raise feelings of horror and indignation in the country'.

Was Colonel Crawley guilty, as charged? Was Sergeant-Major Lilley an habitual heavy drinker? Is it possible to arrive at a considered opinion by a study of the evidence and what it reveals about those concerned in the Mhow affair?

Colonel Crawley, son of a veteran of the Peninsular War, joined the army as an ensign at the age of sixteen in 1834. Eight years later he was a lieutenant; another twelve years and he became a captain. He took part in one or two actions during the Indian Mutiny, being an extra aide-de-camp to Sir Henry Dundas, commander of the Bombay division. Crawley 'was present' in this capacity but seems to have played no real combatant part in the actions concerned.

After four years as a captain he received his majority in 1858 and became a lieutenant-colonel—the rank for command of a regiment—in 1859. It was, apart from the latter promotions, steady, unspectacular progress. He seems not to have been a born leader, for he relied upon arrogant aggressiveness and a glaring eye as a substitute for a natural assumption of obedience and the quieter manner that attends such.

Why did Major Swindley, who had only met him as a boy, retain such a dislike for him for so many years? Perhaps there had been some family brush with Crawley and the boy perpetuated his parents' enmity. Perhaps Crawley, who was only twelve years Swindley's senior, had offended him personally before they met at Mhow. Speculation could go on; but whatever the reason for the enduring dislike, it was a fact that may offer some clue to Crawley's personality as well as Swindley's.

Crawley, it will be recalled, found no difficulty in attributing the oppressive nature of the Lilleys' treatment to his adjutant, Lieutenant Fitzsimon. The possibility, as commanding officer, of accepting responsibility for actions carried out under his authority seems not to have occurred to him.

When Lieutenant Fitzsimon's testimony proved damaging to him during the court martial of Captain Smales, Colonel Crawley dismissed his evidence on the ground that Fitzsimon was so short-sighted that he would not know whether his colonel was on parade or not.

It is difficult to find any excuse whatever for this outright untruth, which Colonel Crawley must have known to be so. Apart from other doctors who found nothing wrong with the lieutenant's sight, Fitzsimon went to the trouble in August 1863 of having his eyes officially tested in Dublin. Mr W. R. Wilde, Surgeon Oculist in Ireland to Her Majesty, certified that 'he is not short-sighted, nor in any way affected with defective vision'.

So Colonel Crawley was demonstrably a liar when self-interest demanded that he be so.

Then there is the complete turnabout by the colonel concerning the annoyance to Mrs Lilley. At Mhow, where he publicly blamed Fitzsimon for it, he appeared to have no doubt that it had taken place: but when it came to his own trial, to admit the annoyance to Mrs Lilley was to admit the first charge of unnecessary harshness. Here, perhaps, may be seen the wily hand of the colonel's lawyer, Mr Harcourt. Never mind what Lilley had said: the defence would be that however many feet the sentry was from Mrs Lilley's bed the chick gave privacy enough.

Perhaps, if Colonel Crawley had given evidence on his own behalf on oath, he might have had some difficulty in answering this question in cross-examination: *would you regard the conditions endured by Mrs Lilley suitable for Mrs Crawley in similar circumstances?*

The author's view is that Colonel Crawley was guilty of ill-treating R.S.M. Lilley and, incidentally, his wife; and he did it for personal reasons connected with the trial of Captain Smales (in which indirectly the colonel was also on trial) and certainly not because he thought seriously that mutiny in some form was imminent in his regiment.

This is not to say that Crawley deliberately set out from the beginning to make Lilley's arrest into a physical punishment, but he knowingly allowed it to become so. His attitude when asked for small relaxations of the confinement—such as permission to sit on the verandah—show that he was aware, or had been made aware, of the extremely uncomfortable conditions of the arrest and was reluctant to ease them even in this small way: but he did not dare to defy the doctor's recommendation.

Crawley was conclusively shown to be a vindictive man when able to use his authority to annoy his enemies. He persecuted Smales—irritating beyond measure though Smales must have been—and he persecuted Lilley under the guise of close arrest.

But Fate intervened when, through no fault of Colonel Crawley, he had to move the Lilleys from their normal spacious quarters, in which R.S.M. Lilley might have survived confinement. If this had not happened the last sad days of John and Clarissa Lilley would have been known to few people outside the ranks of the 6th Inniskilling Dragoons.

Was R.S.M. Lilley a drinker? The evidence of Sergeant Mills who called Lilley 'a great, coarse, ignorant man' was not reliable. Mills had been a colonel's man from early days and testified to Crawley's presence on parade during Smales' court martial. The very nature of his evidence at Aldershot puts it in doubt. He went out of his way to put Lilley in as bad a light as he could. Yet there was a considerable amount of circumstantial detail in his recollection of Lilley's being drunk, and it may be that he had seen Lilley the worse for drink on several occasions over a number of years; but never on duty.

The evidence of the sentries and of Mrs Lilley herself makes it clear that Lilley drank brandy during his arrest. His batman said he regularly took brandy in coffee first thing in the morning in normal circumstances. Ardaseer Framjee called him 'my best customer'.

It may be that the liquor merchant's accounts need to be weighed very carefully before complete acceptance. They may have been true records, they may not have been entirely so. What is certain is that Ardaseer Framjee, an Indian tradesman dependent upon the colonel's favour for his continued business with the regiment, was subjected to very great pressure by Colonel Crawley and the subsequent adjutant, Lieutenant Davies. No doubt Colonel Crawley gave full play to his hectoring, aggressive manner, which would have been more than a little intimidating to an Indian civilian in those days.

Framjee said: 'I go to Colonel Crawley's bungalow every day. Many times I go. Many times I speak about the accounts.'

What never emerged was what was discussed at such great length about the accounts. The question to be answered was simple: how much liquor had been supplied to Sergeant-Major Lilley between certain dates?

That the authorities in India, from Lieutenant-Colonel Crawley up to General Sir Hugh Rose, were desperately anxious for any evidence that would get them out of their embarrassing public predicament goes without saying. Whether this high-level anxiety was communicated in any way to Ardaseer Framjee, and whether he, in his own interest, did his best to provide the required evidence is not known. Certainly he provided accounts which showed Sergeant-Major Lilley to be his 'best customer'.

Sir Hugh Rose, on the defensive as Commander-in-Chief, India, after the Lilley scandal had been exposed in parliament, composed a very long memorandum on the Inniskillings in India which was not allowed to be used by Colonel Crawley during his trial.

Referring to Ardaseer Framjee's accounts, Sir Hugh Rose said they showed that during his arrest Lilley purchased spirits 'to the value of 25 per cent more than his pay. . . . I called for returns of the number of sergeants who had been placed in arrest since the regiment landed in India and the amount of spirits consumed in the sergeants' mess during the same period.'

This enquiry showed that during the thirty months before Colonel Crawley took over command 100 sergeants had been arrested for military crime of some kind; and that during the twenty-six months following Colonel Crawley's arrival eighty-six sergeants had been arrested by the commanding officer. In other words, 'crime' among sergeants remained at virtually the same average both before and after Colonel Crawley took command.

Of these figures Sir Hugh Rose wrote to the Duke of Cambridge: 'This I consider to show a state of indiscipline on the part of the non-commissioned officers of the 6th Inniskilling Dragoons, and of the sergeant-major of the regiment, without a parallel.'

The enquiry also showed that Lilley had 'unknown to his commanding officer, been at the head of a private arrack [Indian spirit] fund for the sergeants' mess since the landing of the regiment in India, and that when he died a committee of sergeants was convened whose report brought to light that the sergeant-major had, at the time of his death, a balance remaining in his hands of nearly 2,000 rupees, or £200, unaccounted for: that he was seen by one of the sentries who had been placed over him to destroy an account book shortly before he died; that he was heard, when doing so, to say "Thank God, there's an end to the private arrack fund".'

Sir Hugh Rose thought fit to comment on this: 'The non-forthcoming of the large sum in his hands, nearly £200, his extravagant expenses in drinking, and the destruction of the account book which, if the money had been properly expended would have been shown in the book, subject the late sergeant-major's conduct, to say the least of it, to very grave suspicion. . . .

'In presiding over the private arrack fund Sergeant-Major Lilley gave the worst example to the N.C.O.s of whom he was the head, and the result of this fund and of the sergeant-major's own intemperate habits and of his presidency of the sergeants' mess are seen in the unprecedented amount of liquor consumed by the sergeants since their first arrival in India, and in the equally large proportion of the sergeants who were placed in arrest.'

The enquiry showed that in 1862 alone the Inniskillings sergeants' mess disposed of 791 gallons of spirit purchased through the private arrack fund, 3,457 bottles of other spirits and wine as well as beer of which no figures were produced.

Sir Hugh wrote: 'A long experience tells me, as it does any officer of long experience in the army, that there is no passion so fatal, and yet so persisted in as that of drink. And it is remarkable that excessive cunning to conceal it accompanies this baneful habit. . . .

'It is especially in older officers and soldiers—those of long-standing intemperate habits—that the cunning to conceal this vice is found. It is with them literally, a policy, a system, to drink as much as possible without being discovered, or "getting into trouble" as it is called. This cannot be effected if they become drunk: they drink, therefore, copiously but steadily, by rule. They daily indulge largely in their passion for drink, but they stop short of excess—of drunkenness. Of this, good and experienced adjutants are evidence. They say that no harder drinkers—soakers, as they are called by the soldiers—are often to be found than amongst men bearing good conduct badges. They drink largely and constantly but abstain from drunkenness, which would deprive them of the badge and the means of endulging their propensity.'

This fragment of Sir Hugh's final instalment of his four-part history of the Inniskillings, written on 4 October 1863, some six weeks before Colonel Crawley's trial began, shows how concerned he was to put Lilley in the worst possible light.

He had reported the findings of the sergeants' mess committee on the private arrack fund in a formal letter to England several months earlier, but it was not put in evidence at Colonel Crawley's trial.

In another part of his final statement Sir Hugh Rose said that during the Mhow court martial 'on one occasion Lieutenant-Colonel Crawley was compelled to tell Sergeant-Major Lilley that he was unfit for his duty, and that it was chiefly his fault that the crime of drunkenness among the sergeants had been screened by other non-commissioned officers'.

This appears to suggest quite strongly—if not explicitly—that Lilley was unfit for duty through drink on this occasion. But the proceedings of the Mhow court martial show nothing of the kind. The apparent source of Sir Hugh Rose's damaging statement was the following dialogue during cross-examination of Lieutenant Fitzsimon by Colonel Crawley.

Crawley: State what I said to the regimental sergeant-major, or to your orderly room clerk, to distress them in the way you have described in your former evidence.

Fitzsimon: I really cannot state the words Colonel Crawley made use of to the sergeant-major. He told him he was unfit for his duty as sergeant-major but I cannot exactly state the words.

Crawley: Did I, or not, tell the regimental sergeant-major on many occasions that it was chiefly his fault, as the senior non-commissioned officer of the regiment, that the crime of drunkenness, in particular, was screened or attempted to be screened by certain other non-commissioned officers, and that he ought to know everything that went on in the regiment from morning to night?

Fitzsimon: Yes, I have heard the colonel use words to that effect, but I do not consider there has been so much drunkenness in the regiment. I have even heard Colonel Crawley remark that he had never seen a better conducted regiment, or words to that effect.

This was clearly criticism of Lilley as a regimental sergeant-major, but it was for appearing not to know what was going on among other N.C.O.s and not for being drunk himself.

Lilley himself made reference to his being ordered out of the colonel's office, but this was to show that Crawley was a man of violent temper and language, and was recalled as an example of the colonel's shouting and loss of control.

Sir Hugh Rose, of course, knew nothing about the Inniskillings except what was reported to him and it must be assumed that he wrote what he did in good faith.

What Colonel Crawley reported to Sir Hugh Rose about this incident is not known; it is conceivable that a misinterpretation of Lieutenant Fitzsimon's cross-examination could have caused this innuendo to be forwarded to the Duke of Cambridge; but however it came about, it was an extremely damaging suggestion against the dead Lilley to come from the highest military source in India.

After Colonel Crawley's acquittal the Duke of Cambridge published another memorandum. He commented that both Major Swindley and Surgeon Turnbull had been criticised by the court at Mhow, and on that occasion he had decided to give them both a further trial. But now:

'Major Swindley has unfortunately not availed himself of the forbearance then shown to him. He has not ceased to entertain feelings which strike at the root of all discipline. His continuance in the 6th Dragoons can therefore no longer be permitted and he will be removed from the regiment accordingly.'

Both Dr Turnbull and Lieutenant Fitzsimon were also to be removed from the regiment.

The duke added that he considered it due to Sir Hugh Rose to state that 'whilst I am still of opinion that the character for sobriety of Sergeant-Major Lilley up to the period of his arrest was supported by the evidence before the court, statements were subsequently made to Sir Hugh Rose, borne out by the opinions of the medical officers of the regiment, which explain to me the grounds upon which Sir Hugh Rose made the observations [about Lilley] in his remarks on the Mhow court martial'.

This officially excused Sir Hugh Rose for having publicly attributed consumption of the vast quantity of liquor ordered for the Lilleys to Sergeant-Major Lilley alone.

There seems no doubt that when Lilley died, Sir Hugh Rose, either directly or indirectly, made it known that a most searching enquiry had to be made to find some other reason than the single fact of his confinement to account for the sergeant-major's death.

The reader, of course, knows more about the Inniskillings and about the sergeants' mess than did the court which tried Lieutenant-Colonel Crawley, since Sir Hugh Rose's secret memorandum on the regiment was not allowed to be published.

But the Duke of Cambridge knew all about it, and what was alleged against Lilley concerning drink generally, and the sergeants' mess in particular.

Yet the duke was able to put on record that he was 'still of opinion that the character for sobriety of Sergeant-Major Lilley up to the period of his arrest was supported by the evidence before the court'.

In other words the duke did not believe all that was said about the sergeant-major's drinking habits; although he may have accepted some of it. There is a vast difference between liking to drink and being 'a soaker'.

A further factor, not considered at the time, which might be taken into account when trying to assess how much Sergeant-Major Lilley drank, is his weight. He was described by the doctors as weighing between seventeen and eighteen stones when he died. He was, therefore, at just on 5 ft. 11 ins., a very big and corpulent man.

It is a medical fact that the bigger the body the more alcohol, or any other drug, it can absorb and the longer it takes for the alcohol to affect the brain. The reason is that the alcohol, or drug, is dispersed into the tissues leaving a proportionately smaller amount circulating in the blood stream to bring about the characteristic symptoms of inebriation. For this reason doctors prescribing drugs take a patient's weight into account when working out the dose required. It is almost true to say, all other things being equal, that a man weighing eighteen stone can drink nearly twice as much as one weighing eleven stone before the effect becomes noticeable.

Therefore, it is possible that Regimental Sergeant-Major Lilley did drink regularly an amount which to a smaller man, even one equally accustomed to regular drinking, would be too much to take and remain, apparently, sober.

Colonel C. Shute, the former commanding officer of the Inniskillings, wrote of Lilley: 'I have very great pleasure in testifying to the very high opinion I have ever entertained of Regimental Sergeant-Major Lilley, late of the Inniskilling Dragoons. I knew him well during his whole service in the army. He was for a long time in my troop when I was a captain, and was regimental sergeant-major during the whole time I commanded the regiment. I considered him one of the most straightforward, truthful, and worthy men I ever knew, thoroughly sober and trustworthy, an excellent soldier, and respected by all who knew him.'

Colonel H. D. White, who commanded the regiment when Lilley joined the army, spoke in similar terms of him.

So there is this conflict of evidence as to Lilley's drinking habits. That he drank is unquestionable; it also seems beyond doubt that he never allowed alcohol to interfere in any way with his duty.

It may be that he drank more than usual during his confinement at Mhow, and if this was so there is the evidence of his own words to his wife that drink was the only thing that gave him 'solace' in his misery.

So, on the whole, it appears that the reasons given for his

death by Dr Turnbull (see p. 65) were probably as near the truth as anyone can get.

The author's opinion is that Regimental Sergeant-Major Lilley liked his brandy, and his position in the regiment made it easy for him to indulge it; but as an old soldier he knew just how much he could take and that—on account of his great size—was a considerable amount by ordinary standards.

The trial of Lieutenant-Colonel Crawley cost the country £18,378, including the cost of bringing witnesses from India. Colonel Crawley also faced a large bill for legal expenses.

A subscription list was opened among officers to help pay the cost of his defence. It was headed with a donation of £100 from the Earl of Cardigan of Charge of the Light Brigade fame. The earl was not unfamiliar with the cost of litigation himself, for he had earlier that year fought a successful libel action against an officer who had written a book about the famous charge and alleged that Cardigan did not reach the Russian guns—because his horse bolted with him to the rear before the charge reached the Russian position.

Lord Cardigan, too, may have felt some sympathy for Colonel Crawley in his public notoriety, for as a younger man, before the glamour of Balaklava became associated with his name, he was, himself, perhaps the most hated officer in England—overbearing, quarrelsome and cruel—and detested by both officers and men.

By comparison, Colonel Crawley was a moderate and kindly man; only the fate of John Lilley put him in the same class of public odium.

Like all scandals, the Crawley affair gradually receded in the public mind. Lieutenant-Colonel Crawley returned to the 6th Inniskilling Dragoons.

From an account in the *York Advertiser* of 18 April 1867 it appears that his ideas on discipline did not undergo any marked change. The regiment had returned to England and was stationed at York. On 13 April, shortly before 2 a.m., the colonel paid a surprise visit to the barracks and discovered a horse loose in the square.

He immediately ordered the trumpeter to sound 'Boots and

Saddles', rousing the whole regiment. It was a freezing cold night and as the *York Advertiser* reporter put it:

'The inhabitants were aroused from their peaceful slumbers by the strains of martial music, and the clanging and tramping as of troops on the march.'

Windows opened and half-awake citizens of York looked out upon the Inniskillings, 'on whose faces the street lamps shed a somewhat dull and flickering light, but enough to show that the men were out on anything but an agreeable excursion. . . .

'On marched the troopers, led by their "very gallant" colonel along the road to the Hull road, along which they were marched some half dozen miles when the order was given to wheel and return homewards and to their quarters. These were reached at 5.30. The expedition was ended, but it was evident from the gleaming faces of the troopers, not at all improved by the long icicles that hung from their hirsute appendages, that it had been of a most unsatisfactory character.'

Colonel Crawley progressed in rank as seniority decreed, becoming a full colonel in 1864 and a major-general in 1870.

On retirement he lived in York Terrace, Regent's Park, London, where he died on Friday, 2 July 1880 at the age of sixty-two.

The old British cemetery at Mhow has long been left to its memories; but life, as ever, goes on around it. Bungalows for Indian Army officers flank it; a bakery, a laundry, are part of the background. A grove of trees occupies the lower part of the cemetery, screening the pale sepulchres of an empire's past.

As the grass grows long with the season the visitor must tread with care, for snakes may be custodians of the headstones, the enduring roll of British men, and their women, who died far from home between 1850 and 1870.

In roughly the centre of this forgotten field is a square tomb some six feet at the base, with a pillar at each corner, and about seven feet high where the roof rises in steps towards the centre. It is rather larger than the other memorials around it.

A century of Indian summers, a hundred monsoons, have worn away some of the relief work on the stone, but it still stands square and firm and looks good for another century.

The carving on it remains clear to read:

'Sacred to the memory of Regimental Sergeant-Major John Lilley of the Inniskilling Dragoons who departed this life 25th May 1862. Aged 37 years.

'Also of Clarissa, his wife, who departed this life 8th July 1862. Aged 22 years.

'This tomb was erected by the Non-commissioned officers and men of the Regiment as a token of respect.'

Sentiment has ever been strong in the British army and—as has been observed before—a man may acquire qualities in death that were less evident during life. This may have been so in the case of Sergeant-Major Lilley.

It is possible that he was 'a great coarse ignorant man' as testified by Sergeant Mills, and that it was a display of posthumous pity and sentiment by the regiment that caused his comrades to erect a symbol of their belatedly recognised regard for him.

Or, perhaps, as his batman said in evidence, he was a man who 'used to drink a certain amount but not to excess'; and he may have been, as Colonel Shute described him, 'an excellent soldier, respected by all who knew him'.

Troop Sergeant-Major Garroway respected him; and it was 'as a token of respect', it seems, that most of his fellow soldiers at Mhow raised a tomb to his memory.

It may well be that in that fact lies the answer to some of the calumnies that were spread about him when he was no longer able to reply.

Postscript

THE stigma of the Mhow court martial, and the observations of the Duke of Cambridge after the trial of Colonel Crawley, appear to have remained an impediment to professional advancement for some of those upon whom the duke's displeasure had fallen.

Captain Renshaw was never more than captain of a troop in the 16th Lancers, to which regiment he was transferred. During the fourteen years that followed the Crawley trial he climbed but one step in rank, to major, and he sold his commission in 1877. Thereafter he disappears from public record.

Surgeon Turnbull, whose rank had been equivalent to a major when he was in the Inniskillings, also received one promotion during the rest of his career. He retired from the 21st Hussars in 1876 with the rank of surgeon-major—equivalent to lieutenant-colonel. He died in March 1876 at Clevedon, in Somerset. He was then only forty-nine, so perhaps his career might have overcome the odium of Mhow if he had lived longer.

Lieutenant Fitzsimon was transferred to an infantry regiment, the 62nd Wiltshires. He served for another fifteen years, rising like the others by one promotion—to captain. He retired with the honorary rank of major in 1878, and he died in Brussels at the age of sixty-five in 1897.

Major J. E. Swindley, who made no attempt to conceal his dislike of Colonel Crawley either before, during or after the Mhow court martial, is the only one of the regimental officers who reached a really senior rank.

He was transferred to the 15th Hussars following the Duke of Cambridge's criticism. He was promoted to lieutenant-colonel, commanding the 15th Hussars, in 1874, and retired with the rank of full colonel in 1879.

Swindley was never censured for evasiveness or for being less than honest, as were Dr Turnbull and Lieutenant Fitzsimon: Swindley's fault was undisguised antagonism towards Colonel Crawley and this, unfortunate and undesirable as it was in the regiment, may have been a sign of strength of character rather than a defect. His successful recovery in his subsequent career seems to indicate this.

He lived to the age of eighty-eight, with the honorary rank of major-general, and he died of old age and bronchitis at Thames Ditton, Surrey, in 1919.

Assistant Surgeon Oliver Barnett, who had been junior to Dr Turnbull and was never censured in connection with Mhow, served on the personal staff of the Viceroy of India after the Crawley trial, and later became a deputy surgeon-general—equivalent to a full colonel.

He was appointed principal medical officer of Southern Command in England, and might have risen higher; but at Eastbourne in 1885, when he was fifty-four, he died of exhaustion brought about by malaria which he had contracted at Suakin in the Sudan in post-Mhow service.

Let this story end where it really began—with Captain Thomas Smales, architect of his own and other people's misfortune.

After the Crawley court martial he could see no future for himself in England, and in 1866 he emigrated to Queensland, Australia, with his family of six sons and two daughters. He had had two other daughters and a son but they, like many children of the time, died in infancy.

On arrival in Australia Captain Smales settled along the banks of the Logan River near Brisbane with a view to growing sugar. He knew little or nothing of farming, but he set about it with a military vigour that took no account of labour relations.

He employed kanakas—Pacific island labourers—on his plantation, but he seems to have been unable to get the best out of them, or to have known how to handle them. He never made a success out of sugar planting, or the logging which he also went in for; but he persevered on the land with indifferent results for some years. He and his sons sometimes rafted down the river to and from Brisbane.

His third son, Edward, whom he had sent to Eton and who was aged eighteen when the family emigrated, also went in for farming. When Captain Smales finally gave up his own effort to make a living from the land he went to live with Edward at Jimboomba, about twenty-eight miles south of Brisbane, where he spent the rest of his life.

The true facts of the Mhow court martial were not generally known among his family. A more romantic account was passed down to some of his grandchildren, to the effect that he had been accused of chasing a major's wife around the barracks at 2 a.m.; that he had protested his innocence but was not believed; and that years later the real culprit was discovered and the captain received an official apology and compensation.

A variation on this theme was that he had reported Colonel Crawley for publicly associating with, and driving around with, the wife of another officer.

Both were family legends that no doubt caused an occasional chuckle down the years at grandfather's goings-on in the army.

Captain Smales may have fostered these stories as being less complicated than the truth when his younger children and grandchildren became old enough to know family history. Both legends appear to derive from Mrs Renshaw—the regiment's 'moral and social' question—in whom Captain Smales may have seen, either consciously or subconsciously as the years passed, the real source of his troubles.

And there is the possibility of a grain of truth in the suggestion of the colonel's friendship with another officer's wife. Colonel Crawley's defence of Mrs Renshaw against the criticisms of Captain Smales and Dr Turnbull may not have been entirely due to a disinterested broadness of mind on the subject of divorce.

Another family legend was that Grandfather Smales had taken up the case of a fellow soldier who had been unjustly imprisoned and, in doing so, became involved himself.

Captain Smales never really settled down to anything in Australia. At one time he became enthusiastic about a political career and stood for parliament: but his enthusiasm was not shared by the electorate and he lost his £25 candidate's deposit.

He was most indignant at this lack of support and wrote a number of strong letters to the newspapers. But nothing more came of his political ambitions.

No doubt he lived with his memories of grander times in the army. His wife died comparatively young, possibly worn out with child-bearing and almost certainly by the rough pioneering life for which she was totally unsuited either by upbringing or experience.

Captain Smales married again within a year of his own death. He was seventy-six and his bride's name was Ann Maclean. Nothing is known of this late venture into matrimony by the captain, and it seems possible that he courted the lady during trips he made from time to time from his son's home at Jimboomba. He used to go visiting, and there was some mystery about where he went: but beyond that no more can be said.

Captain Thomas Smales died in February 1888 at Sandgate, Caboolture, near Brisbane. He was then seventy-seven and his death certificate records that he died of 'faulty action of heart'.

He had always been going to write a book about his life in India and, indeed, he was frequently seen writing in the house at Jimboomba. But no autobiographical notes were found among his papers.

Bibliography

Cornhill Magazine November 1863. Article by J. Omnium
Proceedings of court martial of Captain Thomas Smales
Proceedings of court martial of Lieut.-Col. T. R. Crawley (Accounts & Papers 1864 XXXV)
Hansard parliamentary debates
Contemporary British and Indian newspapers
The Army Lists
War Office correspondence with Indian Army headquarters etc. (W.O. 33/13 P.R.O.)
Record of the Inniskilling Dragoons by Major E. S. Jackson. A. L. Humphreys, London, 1909
Somerset House births, marriages and deaths records

Index